# THE FICTIONS THAT S LIVES

*The Fictions That Shape Men's Lives* is structured around a number of key "fictions" of masculinity, such as beliefs in biological determinism, the inevitability of men's violence and the opposition of the sexes, and proceeds to expose them as wholly or partially unfounded.

Examining the social pressure to behave and experience the self in ways that culture prescribes for the bodies we are perceived as having, this book provides an awareness of widely-held but distorted assumptions of gender. It also seeks to put men into a position to resist masculine social pressures when conforming to them conflicts with important life goals or values and/or causes harm. Making use of an informal, storytelling style provides an accessibility to those interested in breaking down their preconceptions of gender and masculinity, as well making links to key theories and concepts.

This is a lively and engaging book for introducing undergraduates to the study of Gender, Sexuality and Masculinity courses.

**Christopher Kilmartin** is an emeritus college professor, author, stand-up comedian, actor, playwright, consultant and professional psychologist. He holds a Ph.D. in Counseling Psychology. He has written five books on men and gender, some in multiple editions. Drawing on his background as a professional stand-up comedian, Dr. Kilmartin wrote and acted in a solo theatre performance on men's issues entitled "Crimes Against Nature," an integration of his scholarly and performing interests, which has toured to over 150 campuses and other venues. Dr. Kilmartin served as a consultant for three years with the United States Naval Academy in sexual assault and harassment prevention. He was Distinguished Visiting Professor at the United States Air Force Academy in 2013/14. In 2007, he was the Fulbright Distinguished Chair in Gender Studies at the University of Klagenfurt, Austria. He is an internationally-recognized expert on gender, violence prevention, diversity, and inclusion.

# THE FICTIONS THAT SHAPE MEN'S LIVES

*Christopher Kilmartin*

LONDON AND NEW YORK

First published 2021
by Routledge
2 Park Square, Milton Park, Abingdon, Oxon OX14 4RN

and by Routledge
52 Vanderbilt Avenue, New York, NY 10017

*Routledge is an imprint of the Taylor & Francis Group, an informa business*

© 2021 Christopher Kilmartin

The right of Christopher Kilmartin to be identified as author of this work has been asserted by him in accordance with sections 77 and 78 of the Copyright, Designs and Patents Act 1988.

All rights reserved. No part of this book may be reprinted or reproduced or utilized in any form or by any electronic, mechanical, or other means, now known or hereafter invented, including photocopying and recording, or in any information storage or retrieval system, without permission in writing from the publishers.

*Trademark notice*: Product or corporate names may be trademarks or registered trademarks, and are used only for identification and explanation without intent to infringe.

*British Library Cataloguing in Publication Data*
A catalogue record for this book is available from the British Library

*Library of Congress Cataloging-in-Publication Data*
A catalog record has been requested for this book

ISBN: 978-0-367-42114-4 (hbk)
ISBN: 978-0-367-42113-7 (pbk)
ISBN: 978-0-367-82188-3 (ebk)

Typeset in Bembo
by Taylor & Francis Books

**For Allyson**

# CONTENTS

| | | |
|---|---|---|
| *Acknowledgements* | | *viii* |
| *Preface* | | *ix* |
| 1 | Frameworks: What is gender, and why does it matter? | 1 |
| 2 | "Opposite sex": The fiction of difference | 11 |
| 3 | Blue genes: The fiction of biological determinism | 36 |
| 4 | Mirrors of the soul: The fiction that appearance is reality | 49 |
| 5 | Good old days: The fiction of the bygone romantic era | 67 |
| 6 | A man's gotta do what a man's gotta do: The fiction of violence | 75 |
| 7 | The last action hero: The fiction of masculine mystique | 97 |
| 8 | Onward through the fog: The future of masculinities | 109 |
| *References* | | *127* |
| *Index* | | *135* |

# ACKNOWLEDGEMENTS

This book has been a lengthy project, and along the way, many people have supported, inspired, assisted, and sustained my work. Listed in no particular order, I am grateful to: Jin Auh, Michael Addis, Fred Rabinowitz, Erin O'Brien, Melanie Dulcetta, Dave Westmoreland, Terri Morse, Gary Packard, Amanda Metcalfe, Lynne Revo-Cohen, Gwen Crider, Ron Levant, Adrienne Lawrence, Rich McConchie, Eric Lindholm, Whitey Jaquith, Marcel Rotter, John Siegler, Kenn Briggs, David McCone, Leah Pound, Mike Gellar, Meribeth Persson, Tommy Shultz, Susan Shultz, Gil Wadsworth, Utta Isop, Kristen Mertlisch, Sandra Bem, Alan Berkowitz, Alan McEvoy, Jim O'Neil, Lisa Speidel, Hope Hills, Brenda Hawks, Miriam Liss, John Morello, Drew Gallagher, Jackson Katz, John Lynch, Gail Dines, Elinor Burkett, Susan Basow, Lilia Cortina, David Lisak, Dennis Hoover, Anne Munch, Bernie Chirico, Andrew Irwin-Smiler, Julie Allison, James Nelson, Shawn Maxam, Will Courtenay, Rich Ramsey, Neil Irvin, Jim Mahalik, Barry Shapiro, Joe Ehrmann, Rebecca Campbell, Mary Koss, Jerry Novak, Jackie White, Bob Geffner, Alan Kazdin, Don McPherson, Carole Corcoran, Debbie Mahlstedt, John Hill, Chris McClernon, Christine Cole, Mark Stevens, Carol Tavris, Elliot Aronson, Robert Sapolsky, Calvin Llarena, Matt Genuchi, Ben Murrie, Ryan McKelley, Ryon McDermott, Tara Misra, Barbara Cyr-Roman, Natalie Angier, Judy Rosenstein, Karen Gentile, Sharon Subotta, Erin Boggs, Dave Kolar, Ginny Fuqua, Erin Doss, Peter Glick, Susan Fiske, Laurie Rudman, Joseph Pleck, Alison Green, Tempe Smith, Mike Kuchler, Erin Boggs, Callum Watson, Harriotte Makfinsky, Cordelia Fine, Lise Eliot, Aiko Iris, Miriam Fugfugosh, Robin Semelsberger, Sarah Dye, Sarah Murnen, Shawn Burn, Genevieve Brackins, Frans de Waal, John Foubert, Gail Stern, Christian Murphy, Charles Girard, Makiko Deguchi, Everett Worthington, Lori Daniels, and, of course, the love of my life, Allyson Poska.

# PREFACE

It is day one in my Psychology of Men class. The first task is to describe the "defaults," to name the pressures that the mainstream culture exerts on men and boys. The best way I know how to do so is with an exercise created by activist Paul Kivel (1992) called the "act like a man" box. I draw a large rectangle on the whiteboard and write the words "act like a man" on top of it. Then I underline the word "act" to emphasize that much of gendered behavior is an act—a performance—and that all men choose to act or not act according to their responses to gendered expectations.

Different men make different choices in response to masculine social pressures, and so our exercise is not to describe how men *are*, since we are all different, but how we are expected to be. And, as we will see, sometimes men are internally different from other men even when they are performing the same actions. The last thing I want to do in this exercise is to reify stereotypes by giving the impression that all men are alike. It is a fun and lively exercise, and students throw out suggestions readily:

"Eats red meat."

"Financial provider."

"Protector," to which I ask, "of whom or what?" The response, "women and children." And then I ask, "*from* whom or what?" The response, "actually ... from other men."

"Has lots of sex." My follow up, "with whom?" The response, "women—hot, young women, and lots of them."

"Makes a lot of money."

"Likes cars." I ask, "*All* cars? A Toyota Prius? A Volkswagen Beetle?" "No—fast cars."

"Loves sports." My follow up: "*All* sports? Figure skating?" "No—mostly football."

We go on like this until the box is filled with a list of stereotypical gendered expectations for men and boys, and then the next question is, "What kinds of things are *outside* the box?"

"Crying."

"Talking about your feelings."

"Liking children."

"Being a vegetarian."

"Wearing pink."

"Driving a minivan."

Next question: "When a man steps outside the box and I want to pressure him to go back in, what kinds of names do I call him?" Again, a predictable set of responses: pussy, fag, bitch, girly man, "mangina." Then I ask, "What do these words have in common?" Nearly all are references to women and gay men, the groups subordinated under a system of male supremacy. As the exercise continues, the lesson comes into sharp focus: anti-feminine and homophobic suggestions and slurs are used to police the boundaries of acceptable masculinity.

Is everything inside the box bad? Is it all good? Neither—it is bad sometimes when it gets in the way of a man accessing useful resources with which to live his life, or when conforming to it hurts someone, including himself. It is good when it does the opposite. And it all depends on the circumstance. Suppressing your vulnerable emotions can be beneficial when the most important thing in the moment is to focus on the task at hand. But, when you are grieving because your friend has died, it can really get in your way, when at that point you need to, as an Australian public health suicide prevention program (2014) puts it, "soften the fuck up." As the discussion proceeds, I ask what kinds of outside-the-box behaviors are useful and in what contexts, and it comes around that you need many of these things to be a good friend, partner, spouse, father, or supportive co-worker.

The overall goal of my career is help men and boys feel more free to step outside the box in healthy ways and to support others who do so. Thus, I am not trying, as some people defensively suggest, to tear down cultural masculinity. On the contrary, I am trying to expand it—to turn the box's rigid boundaries into a semi-permeable membrane that is transcended when useful and available to all, not just men. After all, women also need to sit on their feelings and get the job done at times and they also need to grieve losses at others.

This book is about similarities and differences between the sexes, and interestingly, one of the major themes is that women and men have a great deal in common. The question, "Are men and women similar or different?" presumes an either/or quality to the discussion, when in reality, it is both/and. So why emphasize similarities? Because our culture is so focused on differences that we forget our common ground. This focus so distorts our views of the other sex and of our own that we frequently fall prey to stereotypes and misunderstandings based on wrong-headed and sweeping gender generalizations. These fictions can break down when we really get to know a person and discover that they do not fit our gendered preconceptions, as most people do not.

If men and women are to get along better—and I would argue that this is a tremendously important goal—we need to discover our shared humanness. It is the same goal in ending all kinds of these "isms": racism, ageism, ableism, heterosexism, classism, nationalism, et cetera. We often feel that we are treading a fine line between acknowledging differences and appreciating what we share, but it is a false line—both/and, not either/or. What is it that nearly all men share with other men? What is it that nearly all women share with other women? A cultural momentum that encourages us to think, feel, and behave in certain ways based on the bodies we are perceived as inhabiting and on assumptions based on 1/46th of our chromosomal composition.

One place where we see these gendered belief systems over and over is in the romantic comedy, or "rom-com" movie. In the formulaic plot, boy meets girl, girl hates boy, and boy hates girl, but eventually they fall in love and that is the end of the story. The boy nearly always pursues the girl and his persistence always pays off, when in reality it could land him a no-contact order. The reason for opening with this "battle of the sexes" conflict is to build tension into the plot, as without it, the story is not interesting. When that tension is resolved and the couple falls in love, the film ends. But is that really the end of the story in real life? If you are married or partnered, did your shared story end on your wedding day or the day you decided to move in together? We are so addicted to falling-in-love stories that we have trouble conceiving of a being-in-love story. There is little tension in the latter. These movie scripts can impel life scripts. Rejected men believing that they just need to try harder, and reluctant women believing that they are being pursued because this love was meant to be.

Nearly always, the basis for the relationship in these stories is romantic and/or sexual attraction. But that turns out to be a rather shaky foundation for a relationship because sexual urgency always wears away and must be replaced by a sense of shared purpose if the relationship is going to evolve and survive. The unfortunate reality is that once we get to know someone, they lose a little of their magic. We must learn to tolerate this disappointment and develop a true and deeper appreciation of the person if we are to deal with them in healthy ways. That means that we must watch, listen, be with, and think about this human being whom we are perpetually getting to know. And so, as we will see in Chapter 3, applying a one-size-fits-all formula based on antiquated notions of gender can really get in our way.

When most students enter a beginning chemistry class, they are keenly aware that they know little or nothing about chemistry. But in a first class on gender, students know a great deal, because they have been exposed to gendered arrangements throughout their lives. As I read their class journals, I see many stories about what they have experienced. My task as an instructor is to get them to revisit their stories and become critical of the messages the stories carry. As you read on, you will see that this book is about theory and research, but that it is also part memoir. The many stories I offer are either from my own life or are narratives I have collected from others over the years. I invite you to view these and your own stories for lessons learned, both positive and negative.

We get our stories in many places: the media, our parents, friends, things that we read, etc. If we are to live our lives in fully intentional ways, we must learn how to be critical of these stories and expose the belief system that underlies the narratives. And as I said, you will see a lot of stories in the pages that follow. In fact, the brain is hard-wired for stories. Every night when we sleep, random neural signals make their way up the brain stem into the cerebral cortex, and there we knit them together into a narrative in the form of a dream, making sense out of non-sense. People crave stories; witness the popularity of film, television, music and art. Stories are a way of helping us to understand and organize our lives.

I am an almost compulsive storyteller. Many years ago, I put together a solo theatre performance entitled *Crimes Against Nature* because I had come to believe that men need better stories, as many of the ones that were being told to us were distorting what we believe about ourselves and the world. This book extends that work by exposing these distorted stories and helping the reader to understand through research evidence that they are sometimes untrue and sometimes harmful. I do not wish to write your stories for you, only to help you write them and rewrite them for yourself.

# 1

# FRAMEWORKS

## What is gender, and why does it matter?

Gender is a social pressure to behave and experience ourselves in concert with the cultural expectations for the body we are perceived as inhabiting. It is critical for students to understand that gender is not wholly contained within each individual. Rather it is, in a sense, "in the air" in the form of cultural expectations. It is also critical for students to understand that individual responses to these expectations are widely variable. We all know men who are emotional and women who are not, women who love sports and men who do not, men (like me) who are fairly inept with repairing things and women who are quite good at it, etc. Moreover, cultures and situations change and therefore so do cultural expectations. In the first half of twentieth-century United States mainstream culture, young men experienced strong social expectations to perform military service. By the 1960s there came a cultural shift in which military service became largely elective. In fact, there has been no mandatory conscription (draft) in the last 50 years in the United States, although laws still allow for it and males are still required to register for the draft at age 18.

Notice that I define gender as expectations for the body one is *perceived* as inhabiting. I once had a student who was assigned female at birth but who experienced persistent identification as a male. He transitioned to a male identity with the help of hormones and noted in his journals that once he looked like a man, others seemed to react to him much differently. For instance, a woman in one of his classes began to flirt with him in the hope that he would help her with an assignment. There are many transgender people who make such transitions and for those who do not know them beforehand, what sex they are is unquestioned.

When I first started studying men and masculinity in graduate school, I was focused on the childhood socialization of boys. Parents and other socializing agents are more likely to ignore boys' feelings than those of girls, more likely to punish them physically, more likely to encourage them to fight, and place a variety of different expectations on girls and boys. I had a great professor at the time, social developmental psychologist John Hill, who possessed a remarkable intellect and exceptional research skills. One day, as I was talking about differential child rearing practices, Dr. Hill said, "Well, once you get beyond this 'turkey theory' you will really be on to something."

"Turkey theory?," I asked, and he said, "Yes—The assumption that we get 'stuffed' with characteristics as children like the dressing in a Thanksgiving turkey, and then when we become adults, we come out of the oven tasting like what we've been stuffed with." His point was that, of course, we were all "stuffed" with things as children, but the social pressures we experience in different situations also have great effects on our behavior. So great, in fact, that the power of these situations can almost completely wash out the differences among the people present. My shorthand for illustrating this very important point is this "formula."

$$B = f(P \times S)$$

The "B" stands for behavior—the actions of individuals that we are seeking to explain. The "f" is function, the "P" personality—the characteristics of individuals that account for differences in behavioral tendencies among people. The "×" stands for the interaction (like the use of "×" as a symbol in mathematical multiplication) and the "S" stands for situation. Putting them together: behavior is a function of personality interacting with situation. If someone has a very unusual personality, they may behave very differently from others across many situations. If the situational pressure is very strong, we will see nearly everyone behaving in the same way. See Chapter 3 for a story about my experience of masculine social pressure and my subsequent gendered performance at my local gymnasium.

Here is the first of many of my own stories I will tell throughout—this one to illustrate the power of the situation in a case when it all but washes out individual differences. In my years as a college professor, once the class begins, nearly all students are sitting quietly and taking notes unless and until I invite them to ask questions or make comments. I ask them, "If I were to talk with someone who knows you well, for how many of you would that person not describe you as 'quiet?'" Many hands are raised, usually more than are not. I follow up with, "Then why are you being quiet right now?" The answer is quite obvious: people are responding to a situation where it is clear that they are expected to remain quiet. The students are all different, but the relatively strong situation obscures these differences. Likewise, it would be ludicrous to describe the students as "note-taking" kind of people even though nearly all of them are taking notes in the moment. This descriptor would only be apt if they took notes while speaking to their parents on the phone, interacting with their roommates, introducing themselves to other people, et cetera, in other words, across a wide variety of situations.

Situations vary tremendously and we often fail to take them into account in judging the causes of people's actions. Some men may perceive crying at a funeral to be socially acceptable but may avoid it in their workplaces. In the world of organized sports, we often see men hugging and displaying other forms of physical affection with their teammates but they may eschew these behaviors elsewhere. Each man constantly comes to points in their everyday experiences where they must decide what levels of conformity and resistance to masculine expectations they will perform. Some seem like walking stereotypes; others like the epitomes of anti-stereotypes.

Is it always bad to conform and always good to resist? No, and no. The consequences of conforming to masculine social pressure or resisting it run the entire continuum from positive to innocuous to downright fatal, depending on the situation. For example, men are often expected to "get the job done" regardless of how they feel. At times, conforming to this pressure can help them be effective workers; at others it may involve unethical behavior in the service of task completion, such as sabotaging a competitor's work. Extreme compliance to this expectation could result in "workaholism" in which men neglect their families and their physical and mental health by focusing solely on work.

There has been a good deal of recent discourse suggesting that, when we engage in a critical examination of masculinity around its sometimes negative effects, we are implying that men themselves are toxic and damaged. Michael Addis and Ethan Hoffman (2020) eloquently sum up the reason for studying masculinity:

> *taking a critical stance toward the effects of masculinity in men's lives is not the same as criticizing men*; the point is not that men are bad. The point is that masculinity can have detrimental and sometimes deadly effects when it is consumed rigidly and uncritically.
>
> *(pp. 11–12, emphasis original)*

What follows is the story of how I began to learn to be critical of gendered social pressure.

When I was a second-year Counseling Psychology graduate student in the mid-1980s, I was approached by a fourth-year student, Hope Hills, who was teaching a Psychology of Women course. She said to me, "it seems to me that something ought to be said about the men, but I don't know what it is and I'm not sure it should come from me. Would you be interested in doing some research and putting together a guest lecture on the Psychology of Men?"

My advice for graduate students in similar situations: when someone says, "Can you do [this]?," and you are not sure whether or not you can, you say, "Yes. I can," and then you go and figure out how to do it. It is a very important way in which you grow as a professional. And so indeed I said yes and hustled off to the library, where I checked out all of the gender-aware books on men that were available at the time (both of them). Little did I know that preparing this guest lecture would set me on to a path that would consume my career for decades.

I loved psychology (and still do) but I had never been as enthralled with a subject matter as this one. The first fact that amazed me (and still does) was that men in the United States died an average of about seven years younger than women.

(At present this "mortality gap" is around 5.5 years in the United States; in Russia it is an astounding 13 years!) Part of men's relative longevity disadvantage was (and is) due to physiological factors but most of it was (and is) due to behavioral differences. Men are more likely than women to take physical risks, work in hazardous environments, smoke heavily, not wear sunscreen or seat belts, complete suicide, and the list goes on and on. And I realized that *behavioral* also means *preventable*. I came to believe that my father's death at age 50 and my brother's at age 41 were not, and should not have been, inevitable.

I had discovered that the negative side of masculine social pressure was quite literally killing men. Later I learned that not only was it causing harm to men themselves but it was also having ill effects on those around them. Physical violence, the subject of a chapter to come, is the most important and longstanding difference between the sexes. Most men are not violent, but most violent people are men. Learning to mitigate the effects of men's violence has profound implications for social justice and people's quality of life.

Following my guest lecture experience, I decided in very short order that the Psychology of Men would be my specialty. I am grateful to (now Dr.) Hope Hills for helping me find that path. And then three days before I was scheduled to deliver this guest lecture, I was knocked unconscious in a basketball game, and so I did my inaugural Psychology of Men lecture with a black eye and a large cut under my chin, which also meant that I had not shaved for several days, which added to the look. I appeared to be a man who had been in a street fight standing in the classroom to say, "Maybe we need to rethink this masculine thing."

In the ensuing years, I came to understand that the field of psychology was inadequate for fully understanding something as complex as gender, and that indeed, no single scholarly discipline could completely cover the territory. Therefore, I broadened my outlooks to include the study of history, economics, law, sociology, anthropology, art, and other fields. *Men's Studies* is an interdisciplinary enterprise in which scholars take a critical look at masculinity from a variety of perspectives and scholarly traditions.

Men's Studies owes a tremendous debt to Women's Studies, another interdisciplinary field in which scholars asserted that circumstances and cultural gender arrangements have profound effects on the lived experiences of women, in contrast to the dominant analysis at the time, in which traditional scholars argued that these experiences and identities merely emerged as a consequence of biological sex. These transformative Women's Studies scholars also began to bring analyses of power imbalances between men-as-a-group and women-as-a-group and the effects of such inequality. In addition, they called greater attention to the performative aspects of gender, shifting the focus of gender from something that people *are* to something that people *do*. Inherent in these analyses is the hope that things can change for the better if we rectify power imbalances and give people the tools to resist gendered social pressures when conforming to them causes harm and/or conflicts with important goals and values.

Inherent with the analysis of structural inequalities is an analysis of privilege: unearned social advantages that accrue to members of some groups more often than those of other groups. Peggy McIntosh (1988/2009) published a groundbreaking essay on the topic of White privilege that is easily applicable to gendered arrangements. She described privilege as "an invisible weightless knapsack of special provisions, assurances, tools, maps, guides, codebooks, passports, visas, clothes, compass, emergency gear, and blank checks" (2009, p. 12).

In practice, people from privileged groups can move about in public and private spaces without having to pay attention to the many things that people from subordinated groups must negotiate in their daily lives. For instance, as a middle-aged man who is widely perceived as White (I am actually part Asian but few would guess so from my appearance), I can see people who look like me disproportionately represented among politicians, corporate leaders, and wealthy people. As a heterosexual and conventionally-gendered person, I do not have to worry that I might be terminated from a job if someone discovers my sexual orientation or finds that I am transgender. Both of these practices are legal in much of the United States and throughout many other countries. If I advocate for gender equality, I am not seen as acting from some special interest point of view, and my challenges to the status quo are not seen as nearly the threat that some perceive from people from subordinated statuses.

Case in point: in 2003, a young woman reported that professional basketball player Kobe Bryant had raped her at a Colorado hotel, and prosecutors decided that there was enough evidence of the crime to take the case to trial. Bryant's contacts illegally leaked the name of the woman who reported the crime, and she received more than 100 death threats (Munch, 2013). She then became reluctant to cooperate with the legal process and prosecutors had no choice but to drop the charges. Bryant's privilege as an elite athlete and media star, along with the support of his followers, thus operated to preclude the possibility that he might be held accountable for his actions, either in the court of law or the court of public opinion. He returned to his endorsement work with the sportswear corporation Nike after a short hiatus and his reputation seemed fully rehabilitated. After his tragic death from a helicopter accident in 2020, people who brought up the rape charge as a complication to his legacy were excoriated.

There are many outspoken feminist women who receive messages from people threatening to rape or kill them, and some have ceased their public activism due to fears that someone might follow through on these threats. Thus, their voices have been silenced through a kind of psychological terrorism. As someone who also challenges widely accepted and unfair gender arrangements, I get the occasional hate mail, but nobody has ever threatened me with physical harm. This email message with sarcastic tone that I received in 2014 is typical of what I experience: "Dear Mr. Kilmartin, I have been a fan for a long time but I have a problem I hope you can help me with. My wife and I have just given birth to a child but unfortunately, it is a boy, which means that he is destined to grow up dysfunctional and destructive. What do you recommend that we do? Is it possible that we can trade him in for a girl?" The message was signed "Andrew Dworkin," most likely a reference to feminist scholar Andrea Dworkin.

I have learned the hard way not to engage with the writers of hate mail. I am quite certain that doing so will not change their minds and will only result in my becoming more upset and escalating the conflict. But I will tell people about it on social media and post a hypothetical response, because I know that many people who read it may be influenced. In this case, the response was, "Dear Mr. Dworkin, raise him to be a respectful human being, as most boys and men are, and maybe when he comes of age you won't be too old and he can teach you. P.S.: It's *Doctor* Kilmartin."

A few ways that privilege operates: first, it is often invisible to the person who has it. For example, if you are in the first class section of an airplane, you can remain unaware that there are others on the plane who are cramped, uncomfortable, and getting no food. But you can become aware of them merely by turning around and working to understand what they are experiencing.

Second, privilege is always relative. Your experience or non-experience of privilege depends on with whom you are comparing yourself. Extrapolating the above example in both directions, the people in the coach section of an airplane have a level of privilege relative to most people in the world, who cannot afford a plane ticket. Those in first class have a lower level of privilege than those who are able to afford private jets. It is hard for most people to be aware that having water that comes directly into your house indicates a level of privilege unless you are aware of and think about those who do not.

In a very well-known photograph from 1940 ("Austrian boy overjoyed with new shoes," 1940/2020), a young Austrian boy is seen with a look of extreme delight because the Red Cross had given him a new pair of shoes. He seems to feel like he is completely fulfilled now that he has something to put on his feet. In contrast, former professional basketball player Latrell Sprewell, when asked why he refused a $21 million dollar contract when he believed that he deserved even more, remarked "I have a family to feed" (2020).

When we become aware of the relativity of privilege, we can understand how people are astonished both at the feeling of being privileged by the mere acquisition of what many would consider to be the most basic of creature comforts (e.g., shoes or indoor plumbing) and the feeling of deprivation that comes from comparing oneself with people at the extremes of privilege ("only" 21 million dollars).

It is also important to understand that privilege or disadvantage does not apply in equal measure to all members of a group. Certainly, there are women with remarkable privilege and men with very little. But when you consider men or women in the aggregate, it is clear that systemic sexism exists and wields considerable power. As an illustration, see the video "Life of privilege explained in a $100 race" (youtube.com, 2020) in which a group of people are given steps forward prior to a footrace if they, e.g., had a private tutor, never had to worry about having enough money to pay their bills, and had other social advantages. The contestants thus start the race from unequal positions. It is important to understand that an especially fast person who starts at the back of the group could win the race, but it is obvious that this person is much less likely to win than a person who is in front at the start. And, adding to the invisibility issue I raised earlier, those at the front can remain unaware of others merely by not looking behind themselves.

People often cite examples of exceptional performers from subordinated groups to argue that privilege does not exist. For instance, media icon Oprah Winfrey, an African-American woman who is a childhood abuse survivor, later became a billionaire. It is essential that people understand that privilege is a force that systematically advantages and disadvantages groups of people but that individual members of those groups do not necessarily gain or suffer from that force in equal measure.

My experience is that teaching about privilege can be difficult because it can bring up feelings of guilt in those who become more cognizant of their social advantages. One student reacted with, "Thanks a lot. Now I feel like crap." I have found it helpful to say, "Privilege is not something to be *ashamed* of; it is something to be *aware* of. Nobody is responsible for the station in life into which they were born."

Being unaware of privilege helps people maintain the illusion that we live in a pure meritocracy and that those who are disadvantaged must have done something to cause their own problems. This *belief in a just world* (Baron & Branscome, 2011) is often accompanied by prejudice against the disadvantaged group, which may or may not be expressed in outright antipathy. It is easy for people unaware of their privilege to blame those who suffer from systemic power imbalances for their disadvantages. The psychological justification of gender inequality, known as a *greater status legitimizing belief*, is also linked to feeling threatened when people challenge this inequality. Thus, those who hold these beliefs are more willing to discriminate against women than those who believe that the status quo is unfair. Some even take the position that men are disadvantaged compared with women despite overwhelming evidence to the contrary (Wilkins, Wellman, Flavin, & Manrique, 2018). I critique this belief later in this chapter, but for now I want to examine the ways that prejudice is mentally constructed.

People from dominant groups tend to think of prejudice as a consciously-held attitude. In this form, one has only to be fair-minded, as most people are. But like privilege, prejudice is systemic, and those who are able to see prejudice as a systemic inequality of outcome, not merely a way of thought, can understand it at a broader level. For example, in the United States, white people and people of color use illegal drugs in similar proportions relative to their total populations, but people of color are many times more likely to be incarcerated as a result of their drug use because they are disadvantaged in virtually every part of the legal system: more likely to be placed under surveillance, stopped and searched, and less likely to access competent legal representation or be offered alternatives to incarceration. And the prison sentences they receive are longer on average (Alexander, 2012).

Piper Kerman (2011), a white woman of privilege who had attended the expensive and prestigious Smith College, spent a year in a federal prison after pleading guilty to money laundering. She wrote about her time there in the bestselling *Orange Is the New Black*, which later became a popular television series. In the book, she writes about how her prison experience heightened her awareness of privilege, as she noticed that other prisoners from subordinated groups—poor and non-white women—had sentences much longer than hers despite their having committed crimes that were no more serious. She has emerged from this experience as a social justice advocate for incarcerated people, especially those who are women.

Why do people tend to resist learning about privilege and prejudice? My guess is that once a person becomes aware, they become accountable, which implies a moral obligation to use one's unearned power to make the world a better place by, for example, developing oneself as an ally to those with less power, as Piper Kerman has. Resistance is even more extreme in those from advantaged groups who claim that they are actually disadvantaged by finding single instances of hardships in their group and extrapolating them to their entire experience, and/or finding single instances of advantages in the subordinated group and doing the same.

For example, the "men's rights movement" is a group of men and a few women who argue that feminism is men's enemy and that men are the real victims in society (Blake, 2015), citing, e.g., a purported discrimination against them in divorce and child custody decisions and women's ability to manipulate men with their erotic power. The person who is generally considered the movement's founder, Warren Farrell (1991) co-opts the language of second-wave feminism to argue that men are "work and success objects" and are thus oppressed even more extremely than sexualized women. Farrell has even argued that rape occurs because men must take sexual initiative and risk rejection, in spite of the fact that acquaintance rapists, on average, have more consensual sex than normal and healthy men.

I ran across this line of thinking from a student in my Psychology of Men class, who stated (without citing any evidence, likely because he had none) that he was not admitted to the University of Virginia because he was "of the wrong race and sex." He also stated that he "would love to be taken care of" but that was not an option because he is a man. I challenged him on that point, saying that he was a fairly (physically) attractive young man, but then asking if he had gone to websites in which unattractive and older but wealthy women advertised for dates with young men, and if so, if he would be willing to subordinate his personality and desires to one of these women, which is the arrangement that many women have made in attaching to powerful men. Of course, he had not, and it is also likely that few people in the men's rights movement would offer to trade places with women. Their rhetoric of being concerned for men takes the form of antipathy toward women, whom they blame for men's struggles, rather than working to improve the quality of men's lives.

Case in point: I live in Fredericksburg, Virginia, which is the home to the sixth oldest non-urban domestic violence women's shelter in the United States. Men's rights activists (sometimes referred to with the shorthand "MRAs") decry such facilities as sexist because they do not admit men, and MRAs also (usually inaccurately) claim that there are no resources for men who are domestic violence victims. In some states, MRAs have mounted legal challenges in attempts to close these shelters by claiming that they discriminate on the basis of sex, which would, of course, leave thousands of victimized women without safe places to live and recover from abuse.

In my experience, the claim that there are no services for abused men is unfounded. I have spoken with many people over the years who work in domestic violence agencies and when they are approached by male victims, they provide services to them. But they do not have a specific shelter for men because so few men ask for help, and they do not accommodate men in women's shelters because their presence causes women to feel less safe. However, they will pay for long term rentals in hotels or attempt to make other housing arrangements for male victims/survivors.

I better understood why the discrimination against men contention was, far from being out of concern for men, rather an attempt to assert male dominance by making women's lives more difficult, when I attended an event to celebrate the anniversary of the founding of the women's shelter in my town. Some women in their seventies and eighties who had started the shelter decades earlier spoke of their experiences. They formed a coalition of concerned women who had become aware of the considerable numbers of women abused by their husbands but who had no other place to live. They began by taking these women into their own homes. Soon realizing that they needed longer-term solutions, they petitioned the City Council for funding to house the survivors but were initially told that they were "breaking up families." But they pressed on by raising both public and private funds, eventually securing enough financing to purchase a large house and pay the staff to run it.

Men's rights activists have done no such thing. Women's shelters did not come out of nowhere. If MRAs were concerned that men do not have shelters, they would do what these founders did in my town: put in the hard work of financing and building one. Instead, they have put their energy into attempting to shut down the women's shelter, arguing that because they did not have one, women should not either, thus portraying equality as what they see as equal disadvantage. They live in denial of their level of privilege in everyday life.

*Being* privileged and *feeling* privileged are two different things. Denying one's privilege often takes place due to the misunderstandings that first, privilege means that one never has to struggle, second, that privilege always translates into happiness and fulfilment, and third, that privilege does not come with complications in the lives of people from advantaged groups. The confusion of privilege with happiness, success, and/or fulfilment allows people who are in privileged groups to deny that they are advantaged because they experience hardships in their lives. However, if you are a person from a dominant group who is suffering, as many are, it is highly unlikely that you are suffering wholly or partly *because* you are a member of that group.

Alan Berkowitz (2014) provides language to help people understand these complications when he speaks of the *advantages to the disadvantages* of being in a less powerful group and the *disadvantages to the advantages* of being in a dominant group. One can always find some isolated benefit to being in a subordinated position. For instance, people from menial jobs may not have to psychologically "take their work home with them," as professionals often do. People who use wheelchairs usually do not have to worry that they will have difficulty finding parking spaces close to where they want to go.

Likewise, one can also find isolated disadvantages to being in a powerful group. For example, famous people often have their privacy compromised by being frequently approached by fans and paparazzi in public. Wealthy people who own large houses may have their lives complicated because they must hire domestic workers to manage their properties. Elite professional athletes must work very hard to maintain their competitive edge against others who seek to unseat them.

It is my position that men-as-a-group have many social advantages compared with women-as-a-group, but that acknowledging this power imbalance does not mean that we should ignore men's suffering and struggles. Men commit suicide nearly four times more often than women, are more likely to be incarcerated than women, and are more likely to feel socially isolated, all largely as the result of social expectations for masculine performance which they often accept uncritically. Gender roles harm women and men, in that order, and we need to attend to both of these kinds of problems. Being *for* men does not mean that one is *against* women, or vice versa, but those who see power as a zero-sum contest see women's empowerment as necessarily coming at men's expense.

In the big picture, rectifying power imbalances will go a long way toward improving quality of life for both men and women. In individual and group contexts, becoming aware of social gender pressure will put women and men into positions to resist it when conforming to it creates problems for self or others. I have often said that sending people out into the world without gender awareness is like sending them out without computer skills; they will only become more important in the modern world as time goes on.

And that means, you came to the right place.

# 2

## "OPPOSITE SEX"

### The fiction of difference

I taught for 27 years at a small public university in Virginia that fields a wide variety of NCAA Division III athletic teams. Most high school athletes are not talented enough to play in college, and of course, these small college athletes are rarely good enough to play at higher levels. Still, they are college athletes and are a hell of a lot more athletically skilled than your average Joe or Josephine. So I was astounded when one of my students, Leslie, who was a member of the tennis team, wrote in her class journal that a male acquaintance of hers, Danny, told her that he believed that he could beat her at her sport despite having never played it, owing simply to the fact that he was male and she was not. Danny had not even been a good enough athlete to make a high school team in any sport, yet he believed that his intramural-quality skills would be more than sufficient to compete against this "little girl."

Seizing an opportunity to provide a teachable moment, Leslie was not about to let this challenge go by without something significant on the line, so she proposed that the loser of the match buy a case of beer for the winner. As the match approached, Leslie had a little bit of trepidation. "What if," she wrote, "he turns out to be a natural—a really good athlete—and I end up being the one who's embarrassed?" That fear was quickly dashed. As she described it: "After the first two points, I realized that this was going to be a much easier match than I could have believed!" Danny was all over the place, of course—hitting balls to the base of the net, over the fence, and sometimes missing them completely. Leslie barely broke a sweat. His proverbial tail between his legs, Danny purchased the beer and slunk home. To her credit, Leslie eschewed a golden opportunity to "trash talk" about him in the company of their many mutual friends.

Danny had fallen prey to the Fiction of Difference—the belief that men and women have no common ground. Because males-as-a-group dominate in the world of sport (since sports, after all, were mostly invented for men's bodies), then some people believe that any man must be a better athlete than every woman. Because he had never thought critically about the real comparisons of male and female (and notice that I use the word *comparisons* and not *differences*), he overestimated his similarity with Rafael Nadal and underestimated Leslie's similarity with Serena Williams. As a result, he made an absolute fool of himself.

Danny believed the Fiction of Difference at least in part because he is a cultural native, and the narrative of difference is deeply ingrained in the culture. Indulge me as I recount what might seem like ancient history to illustrate. In my discussions with college students as instructor or guest lecturer, I often ask, "How many of you have ever heard of the book *Men Are from Mars; Women Are from Venus*?" Although nearly none of them have actually read it, generally 80% or more of them recognize the phrase, which is astounding considering that the book, published in 1992, is now considerably older than most of them. The rest of the title is *A Practical Guide for Improving Communication and Getting What You Want in Your Relationships*. The author, John Gray, promised to deliver principles for relationship success based on "gender research" (although there is not a single research citation in the entire book). *Mars and Venus* was on the New York Times bestseller list for 200 weeks—nearly four full years.

Gray masterfully sold gender fictions to the US and subsequently the world public and quickly became an industry. He held workshops in New York theatres at Broadway ticket prices, in which he purported to improve relationships for heterosexual couples. He published numerous sequels: *Mars and Venus on a Date, Mars and Venus in the Bedroom, Mars and Venus Starting Over* (for those recovering from divorce or relationship breakups), *Mars and Venus in the Workplace, Mars and Venus Together Forever, Men Are from Mars, Women Are from Venus: Reflections, Inspirations to Enrich Your Relationships, Mars and Venus in Touch, Practical Miracles for Mars and Venus, Mars and Venus in Love*. Then he published *Children Are from Heaven*. Apparently, we all start out in the same place but at some point migrate to different planets, presumably at puberty. Gray even started an enterprise to accredit counseling and mental health facilities as official "*Mars and Venus* Counseling Centers." The center would pay a hefty fee in exchange for using the *Mars and Venus* franchise name and receiving a set of Gray's videos. Not surprisingly, there were no standards of practice to which the center would have to adhere; the accreditation was based solely on the willingness to pay the fee.

In hawking his self-help videos, Gray mobilized that great marketing tool of the cable television generation, the infomercial. Like other extended sales pitches of this genre, it featured "audience members" who are almost psychotically enthused about the product. In a moment that truly exemplified his approach, Gray is shown telling a small group of attentive men what their wives need from them emotionally, despite the fact that he had never met a single one of their wives! Rather than responding with, "How arrogant! You don't even know her," the men's response seemed to be, "How insightful! You know her better than I do!"

Gray's message was simple: all men are alike; all women are alike; all men are different from all women. Since we come from different planets, men and women have very little common ground. A man needs to "go to his cave" when he is struggling with something emotional, but his wife needs to "talk it out." He needs sex to feel valued, but she needs verbal expressions of affection. Men need to feel ambitious and powerful; women view feelings as more important than achievements. It seems that each of us can only manage 50% of the human experience. Gray goes on and on, and the underlying message is this: men and women are so different that the best we can hope for is to understand these creatures from another planet and learn to tolerate and perhaps romanticize their annoying habits.

The problem with this approach is that actual gender research indicates that men are not all alike and neither are women. We all know women who have "caves" and men who need to talk it out, men who are emotional and women who are not, men who love children and women who do not want to be in the same room with a child, women like Leslie who are athletic and men like Danny who are not. I was talking about this interplanetary theory at a conference and a woman in the audience said, "But I have a 'cave'!" My response was that she had better take a close look—according to Dr. Gray, she must also have a penis.

Decades of careful research from actual social scientists (Gray's academic credentials are suspect at best) have demonstrated that there is great diversity within the population of women and within the population of men, and that when you look at averages, men and women are overwhelmingly more similar than different (Hyde, 2005). In fact, there are many more studies in which researchers did not find a sex difference than those in which they did, and even when there was a difference, it tended to be a small one (Zell, Krizen, & Teeter, 2015). As gender psychologist Sandra Bem (1998) told her children when they were young, "What sex you are doesn't matter unless you're trying to make a baby." To be technical, outside the realms of gestation, lactation, menstruation, and impregnation, the sex of the person rarely accounts for more than 5–10% of the variance in behavior, leaving 90–95% accounted for by other factors such as intelligence, personality, social pressure, or learning experiences.

*Mars and Venus* sold well for a number of reasons. First and foremost, it had a very catchy title, the foot-in-the-door for the book-buying public. There are not too many books of this ilk that can lay claim to decades of staying power in its title. Second, it catered to people's widely-held prejudices about men and women. A tried-and-true formula for gender marketing is to find clever ways to tell people what they think they already know. Prejudice is an emotional thing; people become uncomfortable when you challenge their mistaken beliefs, and so a book that challenges gender bigotry is going to be much more difficult to sell. Although a lot of people will pay good money to become frightened on roller coasters or by scary movies, very few would plunk down $12.95 to have their gender anxiety tweaked. (And I will admit to a little jealousy because John Gray's books sell like hotcakes and my books sell like, well ... fruitcakes.)

Third, and most importantly, *Mars and Venus* offered an understandable, one-size-fits-all formulation for a problem that everyone experiences from time to time: relationship conflict. And it offered simple solutions to complex problems. If a woman is having a rough time in dealing with her husband, she can simply understand that he behaves the way he does because he's a Martian, and as a Venusian, she must adjust. She does not have to negotiate with the *person*; she merely has to deal with the *category*. He cannot be held accountable for his bad behavior because Martians will be Martians. He cannot change; she must accept him as he is rather than try to manage a resolution that involves negotiation. Perhaps the most disturbing suggestion that Gray makes is that wives should submit to sex with their husbands even when they are not interested, since in his assumptive world, all men need sex to feel valued.

On my view, *Mars and Venus* is little more than sexism of a romantic variety: a bigotry-in-sheep's-clothing that justifies one's seeing a biological categorization before seeing a person. There is a certain irony that the author of *Mars and Venus* is named Gray when he paints nearly everything in black-and-white.

Comedian Rob Becker was the John Gray of solo theatre performance. In 1991, he began doing a comedy club act entitled *Defending the Caveman*. The show was highly successful and progressed to Broadway theatres and other large venues around the United States. *Caveman* continued to tour for several more years with other actors doing Becker's script. The show's website estimates that 2 million people have seen it.

The central premise of *Caveman* is that men and women continue to have the ingrained behavioral characteristics that evolved during the era of the foraging society (which is more than 98% of human history). Oversimplifying the division of labor from prehistory, Becker (who also has no social science credentials) says that men are hunters, women are gatherers, and that sex-specific characteristics are hard-wired into men's and women's brains based on the traits developed through centuries of doing these two activities. When I saw his performance at the Improv comedy club in Washington, D.C., the staff had put signs saying "hunters" and "gatherers" over the restroom signs that say "men" and "women".

Becker uses the hunter/gatherer distinction as a vehicle for comedic situations that follow from mainstream gender stereotypes. For example, men have to turn down the radio when they are lost in the car because hunters can only concentrate on one thing at a time. Women like to shop because gatherers must be able to see the big picture and pay attention to colors to know what fruit is ripe and what plants are edible. A man does not like to shop; he goes to the store and "kills" a shirt. The *Caveman* website states that Becker wrote the show during an "informal study of anthropology, prehistory, psychology, sociology, and mythology."

I found *Defending the Caveman* to be entertaining, a tribute to Rob Becker's performance skills and his clever use of the hunter/gatherer metaphor to discuss purported sex differences in ways that both men and women find palatable. In other words, it was successful for the same reasons as *Mars and Venus*; it reified gender stereotypes and left men and women with a fictional yet romanticized understanding of each other. An audience member gets the same feeling after seeing *Caveman* that a reader gets after going through *Mars and Venus*: "Now I understand why I struggle with this other person. It's because we're so different, and that's what makes love so great!"

A more recent Fiction of Difference pitchman is comedian/talk show host/advice author Steve Harvey (2014), who also has no more scholarly credentials than Gray or Becker. However, unlike Gray or Becker, Harvey does not address men at all. His books and advice are all targeted toward helping women manipulate men, whom he sees as unchangeable from within and unresponsive to anything but sexual withholding and strategic coercion. In his bestseller *Act Like a Lady; Think Like a Man: What Men Really Think about Love, Relationships, Intimacy, and Commitment*, which Harvey describes as a "playbook," he begins by saying, "There is no truer statement; men are simple" (p. 1). To me, this is the height of male-bashing, and it is simply not true. As my friend and colleague Dr. Michael Addis is fond of saying, "Any statement that begins with 'Men are …' or 'Women are …' is wrong," as is this one. Rather than associating being a man with some measure of dignity, Harvey portrays us as being driven by little more than the desires for status, money, and sex. Once women understand these motivations, they can use their erotic power to entrap men into what Harvey describes as a real quality relationship. It is difficult for me to understand how you can have a great relationship with someone who is simple, but maybe I cannot figure that out because I am simple. On the Dr. Phil Show, Harvey told the women in the audience, "You expect your man to talk to you the way you talk to him. We can't do it! We're not wired that way." Translation: lower your expectations and accept men's emotional and relational inattentiveness as something you cannot change. I was waiting for the neuroscience to back up that claim; it was not forthcoming.

One of Harvey's proposals that got the most attention was the "90-day rule." He advises a woman that she should not have sex with a man until they have been dating for three months. He likens this arrangement to having to work for a company for 90 days before being eligible for benefits such as health insurance, profit sharing, paid vacation, etc., and stated that women "have the greatest benefit of all." And so, he characterizes sex is a commodity that men *get* and women *give up*. Insulting to women; insulting to men, and not very respectful of women's sexual agency.

Even worse, in 2012 Kara King self-published *The Power of the Pussy: How to Get What You Want from Men: Love, Respect, Commitment and More*, which again paints men with the undignified sense of being driven by little more than sex and assigns women the task of manipulating men by using their erotic power in strategic ways, which to me, as with Harvey's 90-day rule, takes away an important part of women's sexual decision making, as she has to continually evaluate whether she is either giving or withholding too much. The top of the front cover reads, "If men are dogs, this is animal control." So, this book appears to be written for the woman who wants to have a relationship with a dog.

I pause here to write a few words about so-called "male-bashing," rhetoric that is considered insulting to men. Rarely applied to statements like "men are simple," or "men are dogs," people are much more likely to level the male-bashing charge against feminist critiques of sexism and male supremacy. I think that this is a valid claim if the speaker is suggesting that all men are inherently sexist and domineering. As a man, I do not much care for the suggestion that all men are bad, but I understand where it comes from when a woman who experiences sexism on a daily basis expresses her frustration by denigrating men as a group. And, more than being merely an individually-held characteristic, sexism is a system that creates serious problems for women and men, in that order. Much more on this later.

Often accompanied by the belief that men are simple is the assertion that women are morally superior to men. One of the most frequent quoted lines from novelist William Golding is, "I think women are foolish to pretend that they are equal to men. They are far superior and always have been" (see youtube.com, 2019). We can see what Golding thinks about males from his most well-known novel, *Lord of the Flies*. A group of British boys are marooned on a desert island and, rather than banding together to help one another survive, they form tribes and engage in violent clashes, at least one of which involves murder. I have seen Golding's quote about women's superiority quite a few times on social media, and the intention seems to be to praise women. However, in the process, Golding, much like Steve Harvey, is denigrating men.

A somewhat less insulting suggestion that men cannot be counted on to behave in respectful ways is the myth of the male "midlife crisis," an idea first proposed by therapist Elliott Jaques (1965) and popularized by two bestselling books of the 1970s (Levinson et al., 1978; Sheehy, 1976). The belief that this crisis is a predictable stage of a man's life persists to the present day. Theoretically, the crisis is a reaction to the physical decline of aging and the regrets that men have about their career and relationship choices. In response, middle-aged men embark on a quest to recapture a feeling of youthfulness. Stereotypical behaviors in this endeavor might include quitting a job, buying a sports car, getting divorced, or engaging in physically risky sports. However, although some men (as well as some women) experience a crisis at that time, most people negotiate the challenges that come with mid-life effectively and without anything that resembles a crisis (Infurna, Gerstorf, & Lachman, 2020), and of course, some people have crises at other times of life as well.

If it is largely untrue, why does the myth of the male mid-life crisis persist? First, it is a frequent topic for jokes, television and movie plots, and gossip. Second, although we know that seeing is believing, we also know that believing is seeing. If I know a man who seems to suddenly abdicate his responsibilities and behave in stereotypically outlandish ways at this age and I subscribe to the myth, I may fail to notice that the vast majority of middle aged men I know are going on with their lives without such drama. Later in this chapter I will explain in more detail how this *confirmation bias* emerges. For now, suffice it to say that it is often quite difficult to notice and remember what people are *not* doing. The myth of the male mid-life crisis is a gentler form of "male-bashing" because it is the suggestion that men of a certain age cannot be counted on to consider the impact of their behavior on themselves and others.

For me, "male-bashing" has a dimension that is a much bigger problem than its insulting nature: it lets us off the hook. Some believe that men in midlife cannot take responsibility seriously and are therefore not to be held accountable for their erratic behavior. If we are simple, naturally sexist, intractably violent, out-of-control, etc., then whose task is it to make the world a better place? Not us—we are incapable of this kind of work. I think that we have to see men as complex, moral, and dignified to solve many modern-day problems, and we have to get beyond the fiction of difference to do so by learning to conceptualize women and men as being on the same team.

Importantly, Gray, Becker, Harvey, King, and others of their ilk locate the source of gender in some vague biological essence, and so they downplay the individual's responsibility for their own actions. If a man becomes sullen and uncommunicative, his wife might view his actions as reflecting a willful and manipulative emotional withdrawal. But if she goes to a John Gray seminar, she will understand that a man "needs" to go to his "cave" and be left alone when he has a problem. If she sees *Caveman*, she will understand that, because hunters can only focus on one thing at a time, her husband cannot possibly have any time for her if he has anything else on his mind at the time. If she reads *Act Like a Lady*, she will understand that men are simple and cannot grasp the nuances of intimate relationships. The messages are identical: All men are alike. All women are alike. All men are different from all women. Therefore, the best we can do is to relinquish the expectation that our partners might be able to respond to us by understanding our points of view and behaving in cooperative ways. I have more faith in men than that.

Importantly, the Gray-Becker-Harvey-King paradigm describes a gulf between men and women at a time when, as you will see, it is important for us to emphasize the common ground between the sexes. According to their points of view, if you are angry or disappointed with your partner's behavior, it is not because they are behaving badly. It is because you come from a certain planet (or brain structure) and have not exerted enough effort to understand those who come from different ones. I think we can expect better than to lower our expectations to the point where the best we can hope for is the uneasy truce between men and women proposed therein.

More Fiction of Difference narrative in mainstream culture: as a psychologist, I am always interested in seeing what research studies make it into the popular press and how they are reported. Two particular instances stand out in my memory. In 2011, the press seized upon a British study stating that 83% of men reported that they had ignored Global Positioning System (GPS) directions, and ha, ha, ha, it just goes to show you that men won't ask for directions. How many women had also ignored the calm voice of the GPS? Sixty-three percent. Sounds to me like this is more of a similarity than a difference, and perhaps we could attribute it to many other factors. Maybe more men than women owned these devices at the time. The average man logs more hours behind the wheel than the average woman, giving him more opportunities to eschew directions. Now that navigation systems are fairly commonplace, nearly anyone who has used them understands why one might go against the GPS Voice of the Electronic Goddess: they or their passenger knows a better way; the route does not seem to exist; the road is closed. But never let critical thinking get in the way of a feel-good news story that will pander to people's gender prejudices.

Sometime earlier, the local evening news in Washington, D.C. contained a feature based on an Associated Press story entitled, "Women Have Better Emotional Memory than Men." Some researchers (whose names were not mentioned in the story) tested the emotional memory of 12 women and 12 men by showing them sets of pictures. Some were emotionally neutral, like a picture of a fire hydrant, a landscape, and a bookcase. Others were emotionally intense, like photographs of dead bodies, crying people, and interestingly, a dirty toilet. Each image was displayed for three seconds, and the participants were later asked to recall what they had seen. Men remembered about 60 percent of the highly emotional pictures; women recalled about 75 percent. Again, more of a similarity than a difference, but again it was reported as a difference, as though men could not remember anything and women could remember everything.

Following the report of the study, the camera returns to the news team and the male anchor quips, "Now I know why my wife remembers every fight we've ever had!" The woman anchor, the weatherman, and the sports reporter all chuckle. It is noteworthy here that few people would tolerate such a line that stereotypes most other classes of people. No news anchor would say, "now I know why poor people are always complaining," or "now I know why Latinos like to dance so much," but making sweeping generalizations about men and women is considered an appropriate social activity because it is seen as just good fun, and even if the study is about, as one of my favorite mentors from graduate school put it, "strange people doing strange things for the shortest possible period of time," anything that tells us what we think we already know about men and women is considered newsworthy.

The Fiction of Difference and other gender myths have created complications in my career as a university instructor. It might surprise you to know that it is often difficult to get college men to take a course entitled Psychology of Men, and it is not because they are disinterested. In fact, they often question the women in the class about what is being discussed. They avoid the course because (and my male students' reports bear this out) other men will tease them about not being masculine enough to be so absolutely sure about themselves that they are questioning how they should live their gendered lives. Most men are interested in the topic. After all, we are talking about an essence that is critical to their senses of self that nobody is helping them to examine. Ironically, since it is considered feminine to explore the topic, many feel that they need to feign disinterest. Many of the women in the class tell me of numerous men who ask them, "How can you spend a *whole* semester just talking about men? I mean, we aren't that complicated." One of my students made what I consider to be a beautiful response. She asked, "Well … are *you* complicated?" After stammering a little and looking down at his shoes, he replied, "Yeah … but I'm different from *most* guys." Despite the fact that this man felt different from other men, he nonetheless sees most men as being the same. In later conversations, it was clear that he also believes the other side of the Fiction of Difference, seeing women as having a large set of shared characteristics that are very different from those of men. But the big secret is that this man is not unique at all. *Most guys* are different from "most guys." The Fiction of Difference is so powerful that people can continue to embrace it even if they feel that they do not really fit the mold.

When people accept the Fiction of Difference, they reject similarity. We know that out-group prejudice is negatively related to people's focus on similarities with other groups as measured by the "Universal Orientation Scale," in which you score higher if you endorse items such as "Everyone in the world is very much alike because in the end we all die," and lower if you agree with "I have difficulty relating to persons who are much younger than I" (Livingston, 2011). Therefore, adhering to the Fiction of Difference is related to a higher likelihood of downplaying the sexes' common ground as human beings.

When asked to complete either of the following sentences: "Men are …" or "Women are …," people have no trouble generating descriptions they assume to be sex-specific. Men are unemotional, aggressive, independent, assertive, and sexually indiscriminate. Women are emotional, nurturing, dependent, docile, and sexually selective. At the same time, people also have no trouble finding exceptions to the rule in friends, family members, public figures, or themselves. The Fiction of Difference is that these supposed sex-specific characteristics apply in across-the-board fashion to men and women, when in reality more than 40 years of research paints a very different picture. Nearly everyone is a complex combination of typicality and atypicality.

Like a typical man, I love playing golf, and any man who plays the game knows that it is filled with clichés. If someone pops a drive high into the air, someone will say "bring rain!" If he makes a long putt on the 18th hole: "that'll bring you back tomorrow." In all honesty, I find most of these aphorisms annoying but not offensive. But any male golfer is sure to hear anti-feminine clichés from playing partners he has known for years or from strangers he gets matched up with. If a man has a 30-foot putt and leaves it 15 feet short, I cannot tell you how many times I've heard someone say, "Oh, hit the ball *Alice!*" or "I must have gotten my putter caught up in my skirt," or even, "Oh, you hit the ball with your vagina." If the man hits a drive from a back teeing ground and it doesn't progress beyond the shortest set of tees (generally referred to as the "ladies tees"), someone will suggest that he finish the hole with his penis hanging out of his pants to prove that he is actually a man. Never mind that most male golfers cannot shoot under 90 and conveniently ignore the fact that any LPGA golfer, in fact any women's country club champion, could spank them easily on the course. The Fiction of Difference allows for sexism as a social activity in a way that would not be acceptable for many other kinds of intolerance in polite company.

By the way, I never let these comments go by uncritically. If he leaves the putt 15 feet short or fails to hit the drive past the front tee and someone lays out the anti-feminine cliché, I say something like, "Oh, I don't know. I'm guessing that Se Ri Pak or Lorena Ochoa could have gotten it a little closer (or hit it a little farther)." Men who make misogynist statements do so to win the approval of other men. When they consistently meet with disapproval, they will stop and we will all be better off. And in men-as-allies workshops, I always suggest that men who want to interrupt sexism can learn a few challenging statements like the one above, or, if they cannot think of something to say in the moment, just ask the offender to repeat what he said. When you ask, "I'm sorry. What did you say?," the person is much less likely to repeat it without forethought as he may have done the first time. This time, he is forced to say it quite intentionally. If he is reluctant to do so because of embarrassment, the ally has taken him to school. Much more on this later.

Sex comparison research tends to treat males and females as separate populations and compares the distributions of one to the other. The Gray-Becker-Harvey-King paradigm would have us believe that, for most characteristics, there would be large discrepancies in gender-stereotyped areas such as nurturing, aggression, hunting, gathering, desire for sexual activity, etc. In fact, there are four behaviors in which we see these large discrepancies. I often announce this fact in classes and workshops and invite participants to guess at what they are. Typically, people guess things like physical aggression, emotional expression, love of children, interest in organized sports, and asking for directions when one is lost. But none of these answers is correct. The actual behaviors where we see big sex differences are so basic and obvious that people usually forget about them: menstruation, gestation, lactation, and impregnation. Only in these reproductive functions are men and women from different planets. Sandra Bem was mainly correct; what sex you are only matters when you're trying to make a baby. I say *mainly* correct because what sex you are matters a great deal in how people perceive you and what they expect from you (an assertion which the late, great Dr. Bem would not have disputed). Maybe it is more accurate to say that what sex you are *should not* matter unless you're trying to make a baby.

For most characteristics, the male and female distributions would be identical or nearly identical, forming the well-known Normal Curve. In areas where we find sex differences, each sex shows average differences with a great deal of overlap between the curves and a great deal of variability, or "spread" within each population. The conclusions are unmistakable: except for the reproductive functions, the sexes, in the aggregate, are overwhelmingly more similar than different, and within the population of males or within the population of females, behaviors and characteristics are widely variable. As neuroscientist Lise Eliot (2009) so eloquently stated it, "Like every other brain function we've considered, the social and emotional differences between boys and girls begin as tiny seeds planted by evolution and nourished by hormones but blossoming only under the hot sun of our highly gendered society" (p. 252).

Importantly, even when we find sex differences, we need to investigate further to say *why* these differences exist. It is intellectually seductive to make the leap to biology. After all, nobody would dispute that there are basic biological differences between the sexes. But we cannot really just say "biology" and leave it at that. What *part* of biology are we talking about: brain structure? hormones? neurotransmitters? the Y-chromosome? And, how does that biological entity function to produce the sex difference? Unless we can identify the specific biological *mechanism* for the difference and demonstrate that it has a causal effect on outcome, our attribution of sex difference to biology is highly speculative.

Mathematical skills are a case in point, and cultural differences provide a useful parallel. Asian students (again, as a group, with a great deal of within-group variability) outperform US students on average in mathematics. Is this because there is a genetic difference in brain organization that makes it easier for people of Asian heritage to grasp mathematical concepts more readily than their Western counterparts? I suppose it could be possible, but nobody has identified the biological mechanism, and most doubt that it exists. The differences (which, again, are at the average, with a great deal of overlap between the population curves) are more likely due to mathematical training processes and attitudinal differences among cultures. Most people in the United States consider mathematical skills to be the result of natural talent, believing that either you are born with aptitude for things quantitative or you are not. But in many Asian cultures, people consider mathematics to be a set of skills that everyone can learn. As a result, if you are an American who struggles with math, you are more likely than your Asian counterparts to believe that "I can't do math" rather than "I have not learned how to do math well *yet*."

Former Harvard President Lawrence Summers once caused an uproar by suggesting that the low representation of women in the sciences at Harvard might be due to biological differences between the sexes (Goldenberg, 2005). Reading between the lines of his statement, I think he was saying something like this: (a) the world is a fair place with equal opportunities for men and women, (b) Harvard is a gender-neutral institution that only judges people according to merit and has no sexist prejudices or practices whatsoever, and (c) because Harvard never makes a mistake, (d) women are inferior in this domain. I will leave it to you to construct counterarguments at each step.

Summers called for research into the "innate differences" between males and females in science and mathematics. Apparently, he was not aware that there is at least 50 years of research comparing the sexes on a wide variety of dimensions. With very few exceptions, it has not panned out into much more than a footnote in gender studies. At one time, there was a small difference in mathematics performance in the United States. But it has virtually disappeared.

The sex difference in mathematical skills between US boys and girls that researchers cited in the 1970s was likely due to cultural expectations and discrepant opportunities for girls and boys rather than brain organization or some other biological entity. It was not hard to find people (teachers and parents among them) who believed that boys were naturally better at math than girls, and, consciously or unconsciously, they communicated these beliefs in their conversations and other behavior. In the 1990s, Mattel began to market a talking Barbie doll. Among the phrases Barbie uttered was "Math is *hard!*" both a reflection and perhaps a cause of cultural expectations for girls' quantitative skills. In the past few decades, this average difference has all but disappeared with the exception of a skill called "mental rotation" in which an object is pictured and the person tries to figure out what it would look like from a different angle. On average, boys still outperform girls on this task in the US, but Chinese girls outperform US boys in mental rotation.

Here is a good illustration of how sex differences are observed but then shrink or disappear when the world changes. In 1964, the world record for the women's marathon (the 26.2 mile footrace) was around 3:30 and the men's record was around 2:10. At the time, most people believed that this huge performance difference was accounted for by biological differences between the sexes. Fast forward to the present. The women's world record (2:14.04) is still slower than the men's record (2:01.39). But in the last 40 years, the best performing woman is an hour and 15 minutes faster. The best performing man, less than 10 minutes faster. What appeared in 1964 to have been a robust sex difference turns out to be relatively small, and who is to say that some talented woman might not someday eclipse the men's record?

The marathon story contains valuable lessons for sex comparison and parallels the findings in mathematics and sciences. First, there are enormous variations within each sex. By the time the average person finishes the race, both the men's and the women's winner could have gone home, taken a shower, had lunch, and settled halfway into a long afternoon nap. Men are all different from one another and so are women.

Second, even when we find average sex differences, they never account for more than 10 percent of the variance in behavior, with the four exceptions I cited earlier: impregnation, lactation, gestation, and menstruation. Third, even if we discover one of these small sex differences, we cannot know *why* it exists without further research. If you had attributed that 80-minute marathon gap in 1964 to some vague biological essence, it turns out that you would have been wrong, because once we added training opportunities, athletic facilities, resources, role models, and in the United States, Title IX to the mix, the sex difference shrank considerably.

Finally, and most importantly, average sex differences tell us nothing about individuals. Brigid Kosgei, the women's marathon world record holder, is faster than more than 99% of men. Even if there were a large gap between men and women in mathematical performance (and there is not), it would tell us nothing about the male or the female aspiring Assistant Professor who lands an interview at the Harvard Mathematics Department.

People like Lawrence Summers who make these kinds of claims are notorious for their circular reasoning: if there is a difference, it must be biological, and if it is biological, it must continue to exist. It is a way of making biological arguments without actually doing any biology. I believe that biological explanations should carry the burden of proof rather than to be considered the default option. You can only say that something is, for example, genetic if you can isolate the actual gene or genes and demonstrate the effect. In other words, arguments that appeal to biology must describe the biological *mechanism*, not merely tell a story that sounds plausibly Darwinian. Much more on this in Chapter 3.

Why this obsessive search for sex differences? First, we live in a culture that expects them. We use the term "opposite sex," despite the fact that the sexes are not opposite at all. I challenge student and other audiences to tell me a way in which the sexes are opposite. Sometimes people answer, "reproductive functions." Well, they're complementary, but not opposite—you will not convince me that a nut is the opposite of a bolt. Calling the sexes opposite is like saying that a PC is the opposite of an Apple.

Second, and more importantly, cloaking your prejudices in science is a time-honored way of justifying discrimination while at the same time appearing to be polite and socially concerned. Arguments about biological racial and sex differences have been used to justify slavery and to deny women access to higher education and the right to vote. And I am not saying that the people who advance these arguments are intentionally malevolent, although some may be. I am saying that their thinking is often distorted due to their being unnerved by changes in the social order that threaten to empower people other than them. In other words, rather than believing what they are seeing, they are seeing what they believe.

Scholar Virginia Valian points out that there is a disproportional number of Asians in mathematics and the sciences and asks why Summers did not call for research into innate differences among the races. I think the answer is that most people at least know that they are not *supposed* to be racist. Sexism sometimes seems more acceptable. Although I do not think that it is a good idea to start a "which is worst?" contest, sometimes racism provides a good parallel for helping people to understand sexism.

Small sex differences are sometimes used to justify practices like single-sex schooling. It is true that boys on average (again, with a great deal of variation within boys) have higher physical activation levels and lower average grades than girls. A major proponent of separating girls and boys in school, Leonard Sax (2017) argues that boys and girls learn differently and thus schools should be tailored to their differing needs. However, there is no compelling evidence that single-sex schools are any more effective than mixed-sex ones and, not surprisingly, single-sex schools increase gender stereotyping and attitudes that justify sexism (Halpern et al., 2011).

Science has yet to convince me that men's and women's brains are hard-wired differently enough that it matters for social policy, political decisions, educational practices, hiring and firing, or anything else except baby-making (and even that is coming into doubt). But science has more than convinced me of the profound effects of things over which we have some measure of influence: education, opportunity, media images, self-awareness, and social justice. We would do well to concentrate our efforts toward expanding these things in healthy ways to enhance the quality of life for both women and men, who, contrary to popular belief, are not enemies.

We also know that cultures change, and we have even seen gender transformations in our short lifetimes. When I was growing up in the 1960s, few people would have ever dreamed that we would see women firefighters or commercial airline pilots, or full time househusbands, just as it was hard to imagine large-scale behavioral changes in the population like recycling plastic containers or going outside a restaurant to smoke rather than lighting up at the table. Cultural changes emerge from a variety of sources (economics, law, changing social structures, social activism, education, world events), and as people become more gender aware, a new world opens for men and women, boys and girls.

If men are from Mars and women are from Venus, space travel has certainly come a long way. In fact, the field of sex comparison investigation is dying out as it becomes rarer for researchers to demonstrate a scientifically useful sex difference. More sophisticated research measures the effects of gender, not merely sex. To what extent does this person subscribe to rigid gender ideologies, hold sexist beliefs, or report that gender role pressures cause personal or interpersonal strain? These predictors yield much more useful results than simply comparing Martians and Venusians.

Another example of rapid changes in gendered practices: every year of my teaching career, I took an informal survey of my students in General Psychology ("Psych 101"), most of whom were ages 17–20. I ask them to think about their three best friends and then to raise their hands if at least one of the three is a member of the other sex (not including any current or former romantic partners). I would estimate that about 80% of the students acknowledge that they have a best friend of the other sex; this difference even held among the Air Force Academy cadets I taught as a visiting professor in 2013/14. If you had asked the same question when I was in college in the 1970s, my guess is that the figure would have been 10% or less. My classroom surveys provide merely anecdotal evidence, but well-designed research has indicated that cross-sex friendship is on the rise, as men and women increasingly find themselves with common ground, both at home and in the paid labor force. Martians and Venusians are engaging in pleasant, cooperative, and non-sexual relationships.

If the sexes are so similar, and people within each sex are so variable from one another, why do we call males and females "opposite sexes," and why do most people continue to believe in immutable sex differences? There are a wide variety of reasons. Some of them are the result of the human tendency to put things into categories. Some are the products of the way that people seek explanations for their own and for other peoples' behaviors. Most reflect the interaction of these human cognitive propensities with cultural forces that have evolved through thousands of years.

I often ask audiences "How many of you have *never* had a conversation about 'What's the difference between men and women?'" There might be a rare person who has not, but nearly everyone has, and in these conversations, the gender stereotypes come out, often in humorous fashion. "Women can watch a single television station for longer than 10 seconds." "Men don't worry about whether their underwear looks pretty." "Women can ask for directions when they're lost." "Even a man with long hair would never mount a ponytail on the *side* of his head." In fact, these stereotypes are pretty much the entire show in *Defending the Caveman*. Rob Becker reports that, when he told his wife that he had been invited to appear on the *Tonight Show*, her first question was "What are you going to wear?" He found the question ridiculous, as he was focused on other things, and in his show, he of course attributes this disconnection to the fact that he is a hunter (focused on one and only one thing) and his wife is a gatherer (seeing the big picture and being aware of the importance of color), rather than their being two different people with different backgrounds and social situations.

When John Lynch and I wrote the first edition of *The Pain Behind the Mask: Overcoming Masculine Depression*, we were scheduled for a television appearance to promote the book and John emailed a friend of his who had experience being on television to ask for advice. The response included, "Have your wives pick out some clothing for you to wear on the show." This man had never even met me but he "knew" that I was fashion-incompetent (and also that I was married, and married to a woman) because of the natural propensity toward mixing stripes and checkerboard patterns that comes with testosterone and male genitalia. Sometime later during a break at a conference, I said to my friend Bob, "That camel hair sport coat is really not your color; you're so fair-skinned it makes you look really washed out." A woman who overheard us said, "I can't believe two men are having this conversation!," as if to say "What are you Martians doing on our planet?"

My next classroom question is "How many of you have *ever* had a conversation about 'What is *similar* between men and women?'" Occasionally a few people have, but for the most part, the question seems almost absurd, perhaps partly because it might not be much fun—hard to imagine much humor coming out of that—but also because we live in a culture that expects men and women to be different and so the conversations begin with the unarticulated assumption that they are.

When I hear people have the "What's the difference between men and women?" conversation, rarely if ever have I heard any *theory* about what produces these supposed distinctions between the sexes. The gender beliefs seem to have a sort of an *a priori* quality: "That's just the way men and women *are*." But if they are different, there must be something that produces the difference. That something seems to be of little interest to most people. Without any discussion of why men and women are the way they (supposedly) are, the Fiction of Difference becomes an accepted reality rather than a set of claims for which there is considerable dispute.

Seeing is believing, but sometimes believing is also seeing. Social psychologists describe a phenomenon called *confirmation bias*. When something happens that confirms our expectations, we pay attention to it. But when something happens that disconfirms what we anticipate, we tend to either ignore it or explain it away as an exception. A non-gender example: what creates more anxiety in people: getting on an airplane, or getting into an automobile? David and Patrick are a couple whom I know quite well. They live on the East Coast of the United States but recently bought a second home in California. When traveling from one coast to the other, they never fly together because if they both die in a plane crash, nobody will be left to manage their affairs. Many more people are fearful of flying than of driving, yet commercial airline flights are many times safer than automobiles. If people were completely rational, they would be much more relaxed in the air than on the road, and David and Patrick would never get in the car together. Truth be told, there is probably a little hard wiring in the brain that makes people fearful when they get up in the air, as it has survival value to pay attention in those situations. Hunter-gatherers rarely got higher up than when they climbed a tree, so our hunter-gatherer brain probably senses that something is wrong as we peer at the distant ground.

However, the main reason for this lack of rationality is probably confirmation bias. When someone dies in a car accident, we usually do not hear about it unless a victim is someone famous, but when a commercial plane crashes, it is international news. The plane crash is more *psychologically* present even though the car crash is more *actually* present. And so when we get on an airplane, we informally assess our risk based on distorted data and thus we worry more than is warranted by the reality of the situation.

And so it is with gender. We expect sex differences, see them because we believe them, and we often ignore data to the contrary. If we see a group of boys running around and pretending to shoot each other, and a group of girls combing one another's hair and having a make-believe tea party, we might say something like, "They're *so* different! Aren't they cute?" But if all the boys and girls are eating ice cream and cake and playing a game together, we are much less likely to say, "Aren't they cute? They're *so* similar!" or we may not even remember a situation when boys and girls were doing the same thing. Selective memory tends to distort.

On a daily basis, we are bombarded with information about the world, and we need to engage in data reduction if we are to cope effectively with what would otherwise be a cacophony of stimuli. One way we do so is by forming *schemata* (the plural of *schema*): categories of objects or events. For instance, once a child forms a schema of "pet," they can respond to a new dog or cat by transferring what was learned from previous experience with other pets.

Here is a riddle from a few decades back that was used to illustrate the gender schema: a boy is riding in the car with his father driving and they are in a terrible accident. The father is killed and the son badly injured. The boy is taken to the hospital and rushed into surgery, but when the operation is about to begin, the surgeon looks at him and says, "I can't operate on this boy; he's my son." But we just said that the father was dead, so how can this be?

Twenty years ago, few people were able to solve the puzzle, and even today, lots of people guess that the surgeon is the boy's stepfather or offer other explanations, but the answer is simple: the surgeon is the boy's mother. What makes the riddle difficult is that the term surgeon evokes a picture of a man, since most surgeons are male.

I am a former comedian and I really like jokes. There are hundreds of similar themed ones: St. Peter at the Pearly Gates jokes, guy-walks-into-a-bar jokes, golf jokes, animal themed ones, etc. Some of the oldest are the traveling salesman–farmer's daughter jokes, which all begin the same way: a traveling salesman's car breaks down on a rainy night. He knocks on the door of a farmhouse and asks the farmer if he can put him up for the night. In most versions of the story, the farmer says, "yes but we don't have much room; you'll have to share a room with my daughter." Inevitably, some sexual situation arises that is the source of the humor.

Here is my favorite one: instead of saying that the salesman will have to share a room with his daughter, the farmer says, "you'll have to share a room with the red-haired school teacher," to which the salesman responds, "I want you to know, sir, that I am a gentleman," and the farmer says, "Near as I can tell, so is the red-haired school teacher."

E. B. White said, "analyzing humor is like dissecting a frog; nobody is very interested, and the frog dies of it." But here goes anyway. Jokes are all about humor coming from some sort of twist or surprise; we laugh when our expectations are violated and something seems out of place. The twist here is that when we hear "red-haired school teacher" we picture a woman because of an unexamined gender schema. When I taught at the Air Force Academy, two of my women cadets told me that they had gone to a restaurant in civilian clothes and when the check came, asked if there was a military discount, to which the server responded, "Yes, but not for spouses."

Schemata help us to be more efficient in handling new information, but sometimes at a cost. The gender schema is the tendency to group our experiences around conceptions of how men and women are, rather than the virtually unlimited possibilities for other categorizations. For example, I once met a man who told me he believes that "women are controlling." This belief was based mainly on his experience in relationship to two women, his ex-wife and an ex-girlfriend, and complaints that he has heard from other heterosexual men. Note, however, that these experiences only lead to such a conclusion because he is *gender schematic*—he thinks in terms of male and female when he makes his observations of human behavior. He could use a wide variety of different schemata that would produce different beliefs:

- My ex-wife and my ex-girlfriend are both controlling.
- I tend to get involved with controlling women.
- People who perceive their partners as controlling talk about them more than those who see their partners as more reasonable.

- I tend to resist women's efforts to influence me. When I do, they must be forceful in our relationship negotiations, and this experience feels controlling to me.
- Women worry about their husbands and boyfriends who take risks like driving too fast and drinking too much, and they try to get them to be safer with forceful conversational statements that sound like they are controlling.

Developmental psychologist Sandra Bem's magnum opus is her 1993 book, *The Lenses of Gender*, in which she argues that gender schematic people filter their experience through their beliefs about the sexes, but that there are alternative ways of seeing the world that would result in less distortion. Once people learn to look *at* the lenses of gender rather than *through* them, an entirely new world emerges.

Although it sometimes challenges the Fiction of Difference, the science of psychology sometimes also reinforces it. In a common scenario, a researcher is comparing two experimental conditions. If one were interested in finding out whether or not a certain memory technique works, the simplest experimental design is to take a group of people and randomly assign them to two groups, one (the experimental group) that receives training with the new memory tool, and one (the control group) that does not. Both groups would undergo identical memory tasks, and then the researcher would compare the performances of people in the experimental group with those in the control group.

Anyone who has ever tried to publish a research study in a scholarly journal knows the importance of demonstrating *statistically significant results*. Statistics are based on the science of probability, and it is the convention in Psychology to label group differences statistically significant if the odds of obtaining the results by chance are less than one in twenty. (It is a rather arbitrary standard and has recently been challenged, but that is a matter for discussion at the big statistics conferences.) Sex difference research is *quasi*-experimental (not truly an experiment) because we cannot randomly assign people to be either male or female, but the procedure is the same—to compare two groups. However, if I run a research study comparing men and women on some important dimension and fail to demonstrate statistically significant differences between the sexes, scholarly journals would rarely publish it, and so few people would learn about the research. This phenomenon is termed the *file drawer effect*; owing to the place these studies usually end up. Psychologists often give lip service to the fact that statistically non-significant results are sometimes scientifically significant, but in reality, non-significant results are very unlikely to ever see the light of day.

As if these problems were not enough, there is still more that fuels the fires of the Fiction of Difference. I will explore these in more detail later, but they merit a brief mention here. The *fundamental attribution error* is the tendency to associate other people's behavior with their personalities and our own behavior with situational influences. If we see a man cursing and yelling as he drives his car, we tend to believe that he is doing so because he's an angry person or an aggressive driver. In other words, "That's the kind of guy he is." But if we act this way ourselves, we tend to attribute it to the situation—I am cursing and yelling because another driver cut me off or is driving too slowly in front of me.

The tendency to be under-sensitive to the situational influences on other people's behavior further boosts the power of the Fiction of Difference. If you watch men engage in stereotypical sports banter, you would likely think that all of them are actually interested in the conversation, that every man wants to spend every waking hour thinking and talking about sports. But you would have failed to consider that, when one man walks up to another and delivers his opening line, he creates a social pressure for the other to respond in kind. And most of us do exactly that unless there is some compelling reason to resist the pressure, such as when a complementary response compromises one's principles. When my friend told me that "women are controlling," I certainly did not let that comment go by uncritically. In fact, when I hear sweeping generalizations about men and women, I often respond with, "What tells you that?" The question often comes as a surprise and the response is rarely more articulate than some version of "That's just the way it is."

Here is the story I tell frequently about the fundamental attribution error. One Sunday afternoon in October, I was at the local gym on the treadmill. Like a lot of gyms, mine has televisions above the area where the cardiovascular equipment is found (their function would seem to be to distract you from your pain). A man I had never seen before walks up and glances at the football game that was on the television and then turns to me and says, "How 'bout them Eagles? Think they got a chance this year?"

I like sports and have been an athlete all my life, but one thing I became tired of a long time ago is *talking* about sports. To me, the beauty of it is that we can just watch the game, but in the multibillion dollar sports industry, there have to be people talking about it literally every minute of every game, including play-by-play announcers whose job it is to tell us what we are seeing with our own eyes. For the most popular sport in the US, American football, there are numerous television and radio stations where people talk about the sport 24/7, including during the lengthy off-season. And then there are the interviews with players. "Two out, bottom of the ninth, tying run on third—what was going through your mind?"

I will tell you what was going through his mind: "I hope I hit this baseball. I hope I hit it where one of those other guys isn't standing." I am not suggesting that baseball players are simple, only that they are focused. When tennis great Björn Borg was asked what was going through his mind when he faced triple match point, he would say something like, "Nothing. I was playing tennis." That was a breath of fresh air to me, and just once I'd like to hear an athlete say, "I was thinking about the unrest in the Middle East. And do you think we'll ever lose our dependence on foreign oil? And is Kavanaugh really changing the Court? ..."

Another of my favorite moments was a college basketball player being interviewed after losing in an upset and thus being eliminated from the NCAA tournament. The reporter asked, "How was it that they outrebounded you?" And the player responded, "Well, when the ball comes off the rim and you grab it with both hands and pull it down, that's considered a rebound, and they did that more often than we did." Asked and answered.

So, the man at the gym asks, "How 'bout them Eagles? Think they got a chance this year?" and that puts me at a choice point. I could say, "Go away. I don't like sports talk." But that is not what I did because responding in kind was innocuous and because even though I have little interest in sports talk, I sure as hell know how to do it; I grew up as a sports loving male in America. And so I answered his question about the Eagles with some stereotypical banter: "Damn right they got a chance. Defense wins games," to which he responded, "No. Defense wins *championships*." After which he walked away, confident that he had added to the sum total of human knowledge.

My point in telling this story (and I *do* have one) is this: if you had watched that interaction at the gym, you may have thought "Typical guys. Guys—they're all alike." Well, in some ways I am a typical guy. For instance, I play golf. But in some ways, I am a very atypical guy. I am a gender psychologist. When men are performing stereotypical masculinity, they are often responding to the social expectations of the moment. In fact, it might surprise you to learn that, according to my research, most college men are offended when other men make sexist remarks. But they overestimate other men's acceptance of sexism because they are comparing their inner experience with other men's appearances (Kilmartin et al., 2008) (more on this later). They make the fundamental attribution error when they see a friend laugh at a joke that the friend does not consider funny (like a joke that communicates disrespect for women or worse, one making light of the horror of rape) because the only way of knowing that his friend finds the joke offensive is if they have an honest conversation about the friend's inner reaction to the joke. This is a process for which, as you may know, men are not exactly famous for undertaking.

The man from the gym might not even be interested in the sports banter any more than I am. Maybe he wants to be my friend and does not know any better way to make contact. Perhaps he has a lot of anxiety about how other men perceive him and thinks that this kind of talk will make him seem like one of the guys. Or he is trying to find a way to break the ice so he can try to sell me some life insurance. When we fall victim to confirmation bias and the fundamental attribution error, and we see women and men behaving differently, we chalk up their behaviors to immutable gender specific features, and we accept the Fiction of Difference.

There is a long history of the social separation of women and men based on the Fiction of Difference and the lower social status of women, who were (and sometimes still are) thought to "pollute" men's groups or to introduce a sexual element that might disrupt the work of the group and/or the feeling of fellowship among the men. For instance, when I visited Japan in 2019, I learned that women are forbidden to enter the circle in which Sumo wrestling matches take place, at any time. There had been a scandal when a referee had a heart attack in the ring and a physician who was a woman entered the area in an attempt to save his life (Deguchi, 2019).

In the United States at the turn of the twentieth century, "men's societies" became remarkably popular, with an estimated one out of every four adult men belonging to one or more of hundreds of men-only social organizations such as the Freemasons, Odd Fellows, and Red Men. These groups built tens of thousands of lodges that would act as homosocial preserves (a term coined by sociologist Michael Kimmel), where men could bond with one another and get away from the "feminizing influences" that were thought to dilute "true" masculinity. Initiation and ritual were the usual paths to building these institutional male bonds.

It is clear that many of the men in these organizations fear that admitting women would somehow change the very nature of their group's existence, but what they imagine is not articulated in their rhetoric. For example, the website of the Masonic Lodge of New Brunswick states, "Ever since it began Masonry has admitted adult men only to membership. A boy under age could not be held accountable to his obligations; and if women were admitted it would call for such a recasting of our system from top to bottom that little of it would remain standing." It is hard for me to really understand what claim is being made here and no support for this argument is given; the reader is left to guess at the connection between a woman and a boy under age, and how the system would have to be overhauled with an integration of the sexes.

Many fraternal organizations, including the Elks, Eagles, Knights of Pythias, and the aforementioned groups, still exist today, but their memberships include only a very small percentage of the adult male population. Kimmel speculates that the decline of the lodge does not represent a decrease in men's anxiety about their masculinity and their connections to other men, but rather that these activities have shifted to corporations and to the world of spectator and participant sports, two settings that are characterized by a similar measure of male dominance and homosociality.

Although it has also seen declines in membership in recent years, the college and university social fraternity system continues to constitute a significant presence on many campuses, with an estimated 350,000 college males as members across more than 800 campuses. A few of these organizations have abandoned the single-sex tradition, but the vast majority have not. The National Interfraternity Council (NIC) states that,

> Many people argue that because fraternities only recruit men and sororities only recruit women the two institutions are sexist. What these people fail to realize is that federal law has mandated that fraternities and sororities are exempt from Title IX guidelines. Greek chapters are social living organizations and are therefore not required to be coeducational. At the NIC, fraternities and sororities interact on a regular basis. In addition, educational programs and resources regarding sexual harassment, abuse and acquaintance rape are available.

Thus, the Council's position is that practices are only sexist if they fail to comply with the law (Title IX prohibits discrimination within schools that results in unequal access to educational opportunities) and do not educate their members about gender-based violence.

My belief that the Fiction of Difference is carried as a non-conscious assumption is supported by the fact that public statements by the NIC and by individual fraternities and their chapters are remarkably mute on the topic. I could find only one fraternity website that appears to address the question of the single-sex policy continuing to exist in the twenty-first century. However, the question is asked but not really answered:

> Why is Delta Upsilon men only? Since its founding in 1834, Delta Upsilon's membership has been exclusively men. There are Sororities and Female Fraternities at the University of Manitoba which are comprised of women only. Delta Upsilon continues to uphold its tradition as being a men's International Fraternity. We often have events planned with the sororities and female fraternities on campus. These events include parties, socials, community service work and of course the annual Teeter-Totter-A-Thon with the Alpha Delta Pi Sorority. If you have female friends who are considering Greek Life, please direct them to our links to the websites of the Sororities and Female Fraternities.

Teeter-Totter-A-Thon? Really?

Phi Mu Alpha Sinfonia is a fraternity for male musicians and music lovers. The website of the Northwestern University chapter describes the diversity of skills and interests that are welcome:

> Sinfonians range from the most serious conservatory musician to the most amateur musician with a lot of room in between. Membership is not dependent on a preference for any particular musical form or genre, any level of proficiency or study. If you are interested in music, learning about it, performing it, or sharing it with others you are a good candidate to be a Sinfonian.

I found this statement remarkable. They believe that male heavy metal head-bangers, rap artists, folk singers, and classical oboists have a great deal in common, but that a member who is a classical oboist does not have enough in common with another classical oboist who does not have a penis to justify admitting her to Phi Mu Alpha.

The Fiction of Difference was well illustrated in the hit 1989 movie *When Harry Met Sally*. In the course of sharing a long car ride home from college, Harry Burns (Billy Crystal) and Sally Albright (Meg Ryan) have an argument. Harry's position is that men and women cannot be friends because men are only interested in women for sex. Sally believes that they can be friends and tells Harry that she has several male friends. Harry argues that they simply want her to believe that they are her friends when in reality they are hoping for a sexual opportunity. It is a terrifically entertaining movie, but in the end, Harry appears to win the argument because they become lovers. But in reality, Sally was right and Harry was wrong. Again, think of your non-sexual best friends. For most of you, at least one of them will be of the other sex.

I have witnessed the Fiction of Difference when I talk with fraternity members. If I ask, "What does the Greek system have to do with gender?," the room erupts in defensiveness. Generally, men argue that in these organizations, they form life-long bonds. Then I ask, "Why can't you bond with women?" This is when the Harry Met Sally theory inevitably surfaces. There is too much sexual tension to form these bonds, they argue as they ignore the possibility that there is sexual tension among the men. But some of the worst hazing stories I have ever heard involve highly sexualized rituals.

The Fiction of Difference exists because it functions in some important ways. It provides us with the comfortable illusion of a tidy and well-ordered universe in which the roles of women and men are entirely predictable. It spares us the effort of really having to get to know a person rather than merely shoehorning them into some stereotyped category. It covers up the anxiety that arises when we begin to understand that the future may not be like the past. It is unlikely to stimulate uneasy reactions in others whose expectations are violated when men and women step outside of their prescribed social roles. For men, it allows us to maintain our privileged position in the world in guiltless fashion. But the uncritical acceptance of the Fiction of Difference comes at a considerable price to individuals, relationships, organizations, and societies.

Although the Fiction of Difference is embraced by men and women alike, it is especially pernicious because of the circumstances of men in the modern world. Until very recently, men have had the luxury of not paying attention to gender. In fact, many men do not even know that they *have* gender. They see themselves as generic human beings and women as odd exceptions. There is a parallel with people in dominant races not understanding that they have ethnicity and heterosexual people not understanding that they have a sexual orientation. Most social arrangements are set up to serve those in the dominant group. Few parents ever said to their sons: "When you grow up and meet the right woman *or man*, you'll get married *or enter into a long term gay domestic partnership, depending on the laws in the place you live.*" Despite the fact that about 10% of their sons will be sexually oriented toward other men, heterosexual dominance provides an assumptive world in which everyone follows the dominant model.

An interesting parallel to me is the world dominance of the United States. For instance, most email addresses from other countries contain a code indicating in what country the email account is registered. If there is no such code, it is from the US; we are the default and everyone else is the "other." And the country code for US telephones is the number one. It also amuses me when the weather is reported on television and the temperatures all stop at the border. They report the cold temperatures in International Falls, Minnesota and ignore the fact that people live north of there, and they report the hot temperatures in Brownsville, Texas but tell us nothing about how hot in is in parts of Mexico.

A few years ago, my wife spent several months doing research in Argentina and I went to visit her for a week. Every florist I passed had a sign encouraging people to buy flowers for a woman they love in honor of International Women's Day (March 8). I wondered why I never saw such a sign at a US florist. After all, it was a marketing opportunity not unlike Mother's Day. My theory is that US florists did not use it because we do not consider ourselves to be international. We think of ourselves as the center of the universe and only of other countries as being international.

In the gender world, the dominant model is masculinity. The patriarchal arrangements in which men have held sway over most of the world have been constructed and reinforced over thousands of years. Men (as a group, with obviously a great deal of variation within the group) continue to control vastly more wealth than women and dominate most governments, corporations, and religions. Of course, most men are not senators, chief executive officers, or patriarchs of the church, but we still experience privilege as a group compared with women. However, as I mentioned earlier, privilege tends to be invisible to people who have it unless they pay attention. As a White older man, I can be pretty sure that people will take me seriously unless I do something to influence them otherwise. I can see people who look like me in powerful positions. I can go to work and probably not be sexually harassed.

What then, are the costs for men associated with embracing the Fiction of Difference? First, it inhibits us from forming and maintaining quality relationships with half of the human race. Many heterosexual men believe that women have nothing to offer them except for sex or services like cleaning, cooking, and attending to their emotional needs. So it is viewed as impossible to have a quality, egalitarian friendship with a woman. In heterosexual couples, the Mars and Venus scenario results in parallel lives rather than shared experiences, and typically misunderstandings and conflicts arise. Women are now initiating nearly seven of every ten divorces in the United States (American Sociological Association, 2015). The reasons for this imbalance are open to speculation, but I believe that a great many women now have the financial wherewithal to leave a bad marriage. When they are trying to transcend their own gender limitations and find themselves married to men who want to use the same formulas for getting along in the world that their fathers and grandfathers used, wives are finding their marriages more of a burden than a fulfilling relationship.

Some social conservatives attribute the blame for the divorce phenomenon to the fact that women are changing, but such an analysis privileges the perspective of the husband over that of the wife. We could just as easily interpret the divorce statistics as due to the fact that men are *not* changing in accordance with the demands of a modern world, where both members of a partnership generally need to work outside of the home and thus must also shoulder their fair share of child care and household duties. As one Brazilian woman remarked, "Men are looking for women who don't exist anymore; women are looking for men who don't exist *yet*." I believe that men who hold on to antiquated notions of masculinity run an increased risk of being left behind in modern cultures, thus gender education is my "no man left behind" program. Importantly, the Fiction of Difference functions to keep a man in a gender straitjacket that limits his potentials and experiences.

If one buys into the Fiction of Difference, emotions become a nuisance rather than an essential part of human experience. Research reveals that feelings come as a sort of package deal. That is, if a person is "successful" at squelching negative emotions (sadness, anxiety, worry, etc.), they will also cease to experience positive emotions (happiness, joy, satisfaction, etc.). It's a Faustian pact with the Devil. Moreover, the frequent expression of anger, the one culturally allowable emotion for men, is associated with an increased risk of heart disease and stroke after age 50. Accepting the Fiction of Difference in the emotional realm is likely to leave a man at best unsatisfied and at worst, sick or dead.

The business world is increasingly sex integrated and it is going to continue in that direction. Businessmen who accept the Fiction of Difference will be more likely to tolerate, or even to perpetrate sexual harassment in their workplace. The result could be a costly lawsuit, but these are rather rare. However, even if there is never a lawsuit, sexual harassment makes a business a nasty place to work in and results in decreased productivity and morale, and increased absenteeism, use of health insurance, and employee turnover (Lawrence, 2020). The bottom line: managers who fail to pay attention to the common ground between men and women are poorer managers than those who do. It turns out that sensitivity is good business (more on this later). Sending people out into the postindustrial world without gender awareness is like sending them out without computer skills; they are only going to become more important as time goes on.

As I stated earlier, men who become aware of the lies that are being sold to them put themselves into a position to resist negative masculine influences, which are those that conflict with an important life goal, and/or hurt somebody. Learning about these cultural distortions expands men's options even though many may believe that it restricts our choices. But it comes with complications. We might have to dissect situations and exert effort in deciding whether to conform or not. Doing so can feel a lot messier than merely going along with the program. And others (including many women) might feel threatened if we refuse to comply with gendered expectations; they might not want to be our friends. We only put the time and energy into learning new things if we value the outcome. Every man would do well to ask himself if it is worth his effort to challenge the gendered assumptions. But one thing seems very certain to me: it is really difficult to challenge them if you do not know what they are.

# 3

# BLUE GENES

## The fiction of biological determinism

On a flight to Colorado Springs to look for a place to live during my year as visiting professor at the United States Air Force Academy, I found myself seated next to a former Air Force officer who had retired at the rank of Colonel. Once I mention that I will be spending time at the Academy, his question triggers the awkward conversation, inevitable in my line of work unless I choose to deflect from it. He asked, "What are you going to be doing there?"

"I'm a psychologist. I'll be teaching a course on masculinity and helping with the problem of sexual assault in the military. I'm a prevention expert, so we're trying to stop the behavior before it starts."

"Here's what you do. Castrate 'em."

He was only half kidding. How many times have we heard that testosterone is the culprit in men's aggression and a wide variety of other stereotypical behaviors from rowdiness at a football game to the craving of red meat? Following from the belief that men and women are fundamentally different is the fiction that biology is destiny. Of course, our hormones and brain organization clearly affect our behavior, but human beings are also, more than any other animal, creatures of experience. And I suppose we might be willing to alter someone's biology if their behavior is a problem for them or for others (the use of psychotropic medication for severely mentally ill persons springs to mind), but there are not many people who want to go back to the days of prefrontal lobotomy and castration, physical or chemical, to bring aggression under control. Any behavioral scientist worth their salt will tell you that the age-old nature/nurture debate has been well decided: it is not either/or, it is both/and. But ethically, our manipulation of nature is, or at least should be, constrained. Nurture is another story, an opportunity to use our power for good, not for evil.

What do we know about male/female biological comparisons? Here is a fun fact to know and tell, as explained by neuroscientist Lise Eliot in her excellent 2009 book, *Pink Brain, Blue Brain*, in which she summarizes a mountain of biological and behavioral research comparing girls and boys. The genetic difference between males and females is that females have two X-chromosomes and males one X- and one Y-. It turns out that the Y-chromosome, the single genetic factor that distinguishes male from female, is far and away the smallest of the 46, containing only about 60 genes. The X-chromosome has around 800, and the total human genome is around 25,000. Do the math. Men and women share 99.8 percent of our genetic material, and yet we persist in referring to people as being of the "opposite" sexes.

What about testosterone? Men have lots more of it than women, yes? Yes. And doesn't it play a role in muscularity? Yes. Secondary sex characteristics like deeper voice and facial hair? Yes. Sexual response (erection)? Yes. Aggression and violence? Athletic performance? Sexual desire? Now we are getting into more difficult areas.

Is aggression fundamentally a masculine tendency? Following is a countervailing example from my childhood. When I was in the sixth grade at Our Mother of Divine Providence Catholic school in King of Prussia, Pennsylvania, one day at recess (which took place in an asphalt parking lot with boys trying to play while wearing navy blue suits), I turned around to find a tennis ball bouncing toward me. I caught it and threw it back in the direction of the boys who were playing with it. They played a game that was pretty much like baseball. The tennis ball was lobbed in on a single bounce to the hitter, who struck it with his fist and ran the bases. That fateful day, I had unwittingly engaged in what someone considered an abject moral failure: that tennis ball had been in play and thus I had interfered with it. Jimmy Peterson, a giant of a sixth grader who stood around 5'8" (I was at least six inches shorter owing to the difference in our pubertal status), took particular offense at my violation of the sacred game and decided to "teach me a lesson" by beating my ass. I was happy that he at least had an educational goal in mind.

"Did you touch that ball?"

I think it was a rhetorical question; he clearly saw that I had. He started coming at me and there was not a nun in sight to stop him. Panicked, I instinctually pushed him away. He fell and hurt himself. *Victoire*! The fight was over before it started, and I was never so glad to hear the end-of-recess bell seconds later. That is the most recent physical fight I have had—more than five decades ago, and I feel very confident that I will take that streak to the box.

If you are claiming that testosterone causes violence, the first problem is to explain why people like me and the vast majority of men refrain from physical aggression. Is it because they have less testosterone than their pugilistic brethren? Endocrinologist Robert Sapolsky (1997) explores the question in his essay, "The Trouble with Testosterone" (from a book with the same title) in which he summarizes testosterone studies with non-human primates. I recommend it highly, as Sapolsky has a skill that few science writers can match. He explains complex concepts to laypersons in a language we can understand without dumbing them down or oversimplifying. If one eliminates all of a non-human primate's testosterone, his aggression drops to zero (not many human primates would volunteer for such an experiment). Hmm … maybe the Colonel was on to something. But restore the testosterone to 20 percent and the previous level of aggression comes right back. Increase it to 200 percent; no difference. Therefore, changing levels of testosterone within an individual does not result in a co-variation of the individual's aggression, or as a scientist might put it, there is no *dose-response effect*. Sapolsky's conclusion is that testosterone exerts a *permissive effect* on aggression. In other words, you need some, but how much you have does not seem to make much of a difference unless you increase the dose to 400 percent of normal, which, of course, does not occur in nature. And let me make the bold statement that I am absolutely opposed to castrating anyone to eliminate their testosterone. We could also perform prefrontal lobotomies on people and thus destroy the part of their brains that are responsible for goal-directed behavior, which renders them completely docile. I am also against doing that. Read on for more wildly radical positions.

If we had a straightforward testosterone surge–aggressive behavior path, violence would be random, and it never is. Returning to (non-human) primates, it is well established that dominance hierarchies emerge among males (and among females) and that aggression is one path to establishing dominance (although, contrary to popular belief, it is not the only path; more on this later). If you are Number 4 in the hierarchy and you are going to fight, you will nearly always fight with Number 3 in an effort to move up and with Number 5 in an effort to maintain your position. You are not very likely to take on the Alpha or worry about Number 14. There is one exception: if Number 14 used to be the Alpha and he was a bully (it will surprise you to find that most Alphas are not), but he got hurt or became old and feeble, pretty much everybody picks on him, as apes and chimps have pretty good long-term memories, and it is well established that revenge lights up the pleasure centers of the brain. In fact, this bully who was forced into retirement may end up being exiled from the troop and living a solitary existence unless he can find another troop to adopt him (deWaal, 2005). Sapolsky's conclusion: "our behavioral biology is usually meaningless outside the context of the social factors and environment in which it occurs" (p. 158). In a more recent and outstanding work, psychologist Cordelia Fine (2017) also systematically dismantles what she terms the "testosterone rex" myth that the hormone is responsible for everything from risk taking to competition to aggression.

The all-too-common phenomenon of intimate partner violence (IPV), also known as domestic violence (DV), tells us something about the non-random nature of physical aggression. There are a few different types of so-called wife-beaters. Some are antisocial personality disordered (sociopathic) men who are prone to violence in all phases of their lives. Their attacks on their partners are part of a general pattern of aggression. Some have other serious forms of mental illness that manifest in aberrant behavior (note here that I am not excusing them from responsibility for the harm they do). But the most common batterer is the power-and-control type who uses his violence instrumentally and strategically to dominate and intimidate his partner, a pattern that is sometimes referred to as *intimate terrorism*. He is anything but a boys-gone-wild testosterone-flooded maniac; he is a calculating violence technician (Dutton & Golant, 1995).

It is a good thing that the testosterone–violence connection is not the answer, because that would mean that the only solution we could implement is to take boys at puberty and cage them up until their testosterone drops in their 30s. Do not get me wrong; there are some people who, unfortunately, must be incarcerated to protect the rest of us. In the United States, we are especially good at doing so. In fact, there are more people in prison in the US than there are farmers, and more in prison than there are in China, even though they have six times more people than we do. Eighty-seven percent of incarcerated Americans are males, although most of them are jailed for non-violent offenses. Is it testosterone? Not for my money. Is it buying into the fictions that shape men's lives, the toxic aspects of cultural masculinity? I do not think that it is the whole story, but I do believe it is a significant part of it.

In the social science world, the other place where one sees a lot of biological determinist thought is the application of good old Charles Darwin to speculations about social behaviors, a theoretical position labeled *evolutionary psychology* or *sociobiology*. A brief, oversimplified explanation of the theory of evolution: when an animal develops characteristics that prove adaptive, that animal is more likely than his buddies to survive and reproduce, and so that characteristic is selectively bred into the population. This principle holds true for physical characteristics like the shape of a bird's beak or a reptile's conservation of energy, and for behavioral reactions like the salivation of Pavlov's dogs or the flight-or-fight response.

When an early hominid—we'll call him Fred Flintstone—saw a saber-toothed tiger come around the corner (Wait! I guess there were actually no corners at the time), he had to react quickly; either pick up a big rock and try to kill the tiger (fight) or run to a safe place (flee) to avoid becoming lunch. Actually, he could also have played dead and hoped the tiger would be disinterested, which is why, technically, it is not just flight or fight; it is flight, fight, or freeze. These responses are very well documented at both psychological and physiological levels.

We will leave the freeze response out for now but will return to it briefly in Chapter 6. Because Fred needed to act quickly, his brain went into emergency mode without his even knowing it. His heart rate increased, blood was pumped to the large muscles, and the body quickly mobilized to prepare him for immediate physical action—fight or flee. People like Fred who were able to run away or eliminate the threat lived longer and were more likely to reproduce, and so the adaptive response was encoded in the brain structure over thousands of years of adaptation.

The problem with the flight or fight response is that it is not particularly helpful in the modern world. If my student comes into class for the midterm exam, picks up the paper and realizes that they do not have a clue, the same response can ensue. Heart rate will go up and the body will be mobilized. But it is really not useful for the student to go tearing across the Quad at breakneck speed or to jack me across the jib. One of my favorite lines from author Gavin de Becker (1997): "Though we live in space age times, we still have stone age minds" (p. 44). Evolution moves at a snail's pace, and since Fred Flintstone's way of living was all we had for at least 98% of human history, our brains have a lot in common with Fred's even though our worlds are radically different. No serious behavioral scientist would deny that the flight or fight response exists. Nearly all would agree that it evolved because it has survival value, and because that value holds for both males and females, gender does not enter into the discussion in this case.

There is much more controversy about gender-specific applications of evolutionary theory, in which evolutionary psychologists propose that males' and females' adaptations took radically different paths that led to what we now experience as gender roles. In other words, for men to survive and reproduce, we use different strategies than women, a hypothesis based on the theory of *differential reproductive investment*. Put in a folksy way, we are talking about something called the Coolidge Effect, named after US president Calvin Coolidge.

The narrative is probably apocryphal, but I will leave that to historians to sort out. As the story goes, Cal and his wife were touring the same farm at separate times. Mrs. Coolidge was first and as she was led into the hen house, a rooster left his roost and copulated with one of the hens. Mrs. Coolidge asked the tour guide, "Does the rooster only do that once a day?," to which her host replied, "Oh, no ma'am, he does it many times a day." Mrs. Coolidge's response: "Please tell Mr. Coolidge that."

Later in the day, it was Silent Cal's turn to take the tour, and as he was led into the hen house and observed the copulating rooster, the guide remarked, "Mrs. Coolidge asked me to tell you that he does this many times a day." Cal: "Always with the same hen?" The guide: "Oh no, sir, with all different hens." Cal: "Please tell Mrs. Coolidge that."

The Coolidge Effect is echoed in a short verse often attributed to Ogden Nash: "Hoggamus, Higgamus, man is polygamous; Higgamus, Hoggamus, woman is monogamous." The hypothesis is based on sperm being an abundant resource. We make billions (or who knows, maybe more than a trillion?) of them and produce them from puberty well into old age. We have plenty of sperm to spare. On the other hand, women only have one ovum ripen per month, and only from puberty to menopause, and therefore eggs are a scarce resource. Thus, men are motivated to seek the largest quantity of partners; women, to seek the highest quality. What women want to do is to get the best, grade A sperm for her precious ovum. Sociobiologists believe that men are hardwired to be, as psychologist Joseph Pleck (1994) mockingly called them, "roving inseminators," impregnating as many women as possible to maximize the propagation of their genes. The sociobiology evolutionary champion is of the order of blues guitarist B. B. King, who reportedly fathered 15 children with many different women and had more than 50 grandchildren.

The offshoot of this theory is that there is, indeed, a "battle of the sexes," because men's and women's goals conflict with each other. He wants to spread his seed as far and wide as possible; she wants to find a real quality man who will not only impregnate her with his outstanding DNA but will also provide for her and protect her so that her progeny survives and reproduces. But the more he sticks around, the less opportunity he has to knock up other egg-bearers and turn the dial on the genetic copy machine to the B. B. King setting. Now this sounds like the most old-school ideas about the sexes: she wants to find a good man and settle down, he must "sow his wild oats." He is easily aroused visually because that is all he needs to know about a potential partner, hence the pornography industry; she needs more information than what a guy looks like to decide whether it is worth sharing bodily fluids. Women trick men into marriage and monogamy and men are dragged along reluctantly against their evolutionary better judgment.

On top of all this, men are pitted against one another like bull seals on the breeding beach, because they have to fight other males to win reproductive access to the most evolutionarily fit females. So besides not being able to trust any woman, he cannot trust any man either. Moreover, a woman might consort with a roving inseminator and trick another man into taking care of genes that are not even his own, so "mama's baby; daddy's maybe"—the ultimate evolutionary loser is the cuckold. If he sticks around, he needs to guard against the approaches of other spermogenitors. He is lonely, violent, jealous, immoral, opportunistic. I cannot think of a single positive descriptor of the roving inseminator except "dad" and even here he is an absent dad because he is on the road looking for new and receptive incubators. And not even receptive ones if he gets desperate enough; some evolutionary theorists like Randy Thornhill and Craig Palmer (2000) even propose that rape is a reproductive strategy for the desperate inseminator.

Thornhill's and Palmer's book, *A Natural History of Rape: Biological Bases of Sexual Coercion*, was rushed on to the market by no less of a prestigious publisher than MIT Press. The authors take great (okay, not so great) pains to point out that they do not think that men *should* rape, but that only if we really understand the basis of rape can we solve the problem. But when asked how their formulation of rape leads to effective solutions, they had very little to say, which leads me to believe that they really do not understand the horror of sexual assault nor the damage that their normalization of it fuels, and I am not sure they care that a violent few men rape a lot of women. They seem to see their theorizing as a mere intellectual exercise, and worse yet, the book is found in the biology section of the bookstore rather than in cultural studies or some other field. Much of the lay public sees the harder sciences as possessing a body of knowledge with which there is no dispute (unless it is something like climate change), and so it is difficult for the untrained eye to view their claims critically. There is one "chapter" in their book in which they discuss solutions. I put the word "chapter" in quotations because it is a mere one and a half pages long! I suspect that the publisher/editor asked them to include something about solutions so they tossed one off, writing everything they knew about prevention, which is obviously not much. In it, they have little more to say except that teenaged boys should have to take a rape prevention class as a condition of getting their driver's license. I am not opposed to that proposal, but in their minds, how would this practice wipe out millions of years of evolutionary programming?

There is so much wrong with this theory that it is hard to know where to even begin. I am going to leave the rape question for a moment and turn to the differential reproductive investment and strategy hypothesis. Science writer Natalie Angier (1999) turns the argument on its head in a chapter called "On Hoggamus and Hogwash" (after the Nash-attributed verse quoted earlier) from her terrific book, *Woman: An Intimate Geography*. We know that Angier has little tolerance for evolutionary psychologists by her term for them: "evopsychos." But she takes as the starting point the belief that men are hardwired to seek a new partner every night like actor Charlie Sheen or the late basketball star Wilt Chamberlain, both of whom claim to have had sex with more than 10,000 women. Say, just for the sake of argument, that you have the time and skills to bed a different woman every day for 60 straight days. Chances are you will impregnate one of them. Most of them will not be ovulating and some will already be pregnant, and even with the ones who are fertile at the time, your sperm has only about a one in five chance of impregnation, and even if that occurs, many of these zygotes miscarry. On the other hand, what if you were having sex with the same woman for 60 straight days? If she is reproductively healthy, you would be guaranteed two ovulation cycles and maximum opportunity to impregnate, and you would occupy her time so that other men could not. Angier argues that maximization of genetic propagation is entirely consistent with monogamy, or at least with serial monogamy.

Cordelia Fine (2017) provides even more mathematically-based skepticism to the standard evolutionary psychology differential reproductive investment argument. Only about one in 173 coital acts produces a pregnancy, and so the roving inseminator would have to be very busy indeed to hunt down so many partners that he outperforms the faithful husband. Fine summarizes the inefficiency of reproduction: "If humanity were a factory for producing babies, everyone would be fired" (p. 177), and echoes Carol Tavris' (1992) argument that a thorough understanding of sexuality cannot be achieved unless we "reconnect the genitals to the person" (p. 212).

Fine also dismantles the argument extrapolated from the differential reproductive investment hypothesis that males are not naturally interested in raising children, pointing out that, for instance, many male primates engage in parental care, including carrying, playing with, and grooming, and sometimes they even adopt youngsters to which they are unrelated. And, arguing that culture matters even among non-humans, Fine notes that there are differences in these practices among different troops within the same species, the macaque monkey. Thus, there is evidence of the cultural transmission of behaviors within each troop. And although male rats do not do much pup-care, when researchers remove the females from the environment, the males take on that role, a response to the exigencies of the situation. Once again, the social context matters.

The differential reproductive investment hypothesis is loosely connected to a variety of other questionable beliefs about the nature of male sexuality. I have spoken with many women who, when they were coming of age, were told that it was their responsibility to limit boys' sexual approaches because the boys could not do so themselves, as if boys' sexuality is akin to a runaway train. And boys, of course, also embrace this fiction. One of the more amusing (but also dangerous) beliefs is that when a boy or man reaches a certain state of sexual arousal, it becomes a "point of no return" in which he cannot control his sexual behavior (Fagen & Anderson, 2012). The idea is amusing because it is ludicrous that someone should completely lose their mind in a sexual situation, but also dangerous because it implies that sexual assault is not their fault and leads to a blaming of the woman in a heterosexual situation because she failed to control the man.

When I was a sex educator, one of my students, a high school boy, exhibited this belief along with the cultural belief that sex just happens, one often fueled by movie and television narratives where people have sex but almost never discuss it first. The boy said to me, "I was kissing this girl, and before I knew it, we'd had sex." My questions: "Did your pants come off by themselves? Did you feel a draft?"

Educators also undercut the "point of no return" fiction with the following story: suppose you go to your girlfriend's house. Her parents had gone out to the movies, you are alone with her, and you are going to have consensual sex. But when the parents arrive at the theater, the movie is sold out, and so they return home hours before expected, at a time when the boy and girl are deeply in the throes of passion. Not many boys would react with, "Well, hello Mr. Brown. This is a little awkward; we didn't expect you home so soon, but you see, I have reached the 'point of no return' so we are going to have to finish." Of course, he would be able to stop, just as he is completely capable of stopping for any reason.

Men are stereotypically ready to have sex with anyone who fits their sexual orientation at any time, and yet a substantial portion of men report that they have engaged in sexual activity when they really did not want to because they acceded to the stereotype, saw no harm in doing so, were pressured, or believed that it was important to maintain a positive relationship with a long-term partner (Quinn-Nilas et al., 2018).

The belief that male sexuality is predatory and indiscriminate is partly the basis for homophobia, the fear of unwanted sexual attention. I was doing a presentation for a group of people and during one of the breaks, a man told me a story that well illustrated this point. I live in the small city of Fredericksburg, Virginia, which is about an hour by car from Washington, D.C. (this man lived in the Washington suburb of Alexandria, Virginia). Fredericksburg has some small-town charm, and two Civil War battles were fought there, and so it is a destination for tourists. This man said to me, "My wife and I came down to Fredericksburg for the day. We had lunch at this place called Merriman's." This restaurant (which no longer exists) had a small dining room in the front of the building and the bar in the back was very popular with the gay and lesbian community. He went on: "So I get back to Alexandria and I told Jason where we ate and he said, 'Whoa! Don't you know what that is?' And I said, 'Whoa! I didn't know! Good thing nothing happened!'"

What did he imagine would happen? He clearly feared unwanted sexual attention, despite the fact that he was a middle-aged man who was not particularly attractive, but clearly he believed that he was vulnerable because he thought that all gay men want to have sex with any other man. I once met a gay fraternity man who told his heterosexually-oriented fraternity brothers that they need not worry about him, saying, "Yes, it's true, I'm gay. But don't worry; I have standards."

And, one would think that being fearful of undesired sexual attention would give men some empathy for women, who get this sort of attention very frequently, but that does not seem to be the case. Homophobia then, is the fear that other men will treat us like we treat women, and somehow women are thought to deserve this discomfort but homophobic men are not. One story that emerged from the #MeToo movement in 2019 was one man telling another that, "I can't even tell a woman she's pretty anymore." The other man said, "Well, I think *you're* pretty," to which the first replied, "Stop it, dude, you're creeping me out." Clearly, he did not understand that this kind of sometimes inappropriate comment to a woman might "creep her out."

The rape claim is even more disturbing than the natural polygamy hypothesis. Together these theories portray men as real dogs and women as black widows who entice men into their webs of deceit. The available evidence casts great doubt on the rape as reproductive strategy hypothesis: acquaintance rapists have more consensual sex than normal and healthy men, and since a large majority of rapes are acquaintance assaults, it is not about a lack of sexual access (Lisak, 1997). These men are socially skilled, sometimes charming, premeditated, strategic sex offenders who groom victims, obtain their trust, isolate them from social situations, and attack. Moreover, they tend to be serial offenders (Foubert, Clark-Taylor, & Wall, 2019; Lisak & Miller, 2002). Rape is an act of violence that has no more to do with sex than hitting you over the head with a frying pan has to do with cooking. Moreover, as anthropologists Peggy Sanday (1981) and Scott Coltrane (1998) have extensively documented, rape is rare or nonexistent in many cultures. The more that men and women are physically and socially separated, the more gender-based violence exists in the culture, and we see that effect both in traditional cultures where there is a "men's hut" and a "woman's hut" and modern cultures where the men's hut is the locker room or the fighter pilot club.

"Uh-oh, here comes more male bashing," you might say. "He's discriminating against men." As activist/filmmaker/lecturer/all-around-good-guy Jackson Katz (2014) says, "Facts cannot discriminate against men. They are facts." The real male bashers are people like Thornhill and Palmer and the other evolutionary psychologists who seem to conveniently forget that the vast majority of men are good and kind people who love their partners, their families, and their communities.

In 2013, I was very proud to have been named a Distinguished Visiting Professor at the United States Air Force Academy, a one-year appointment in the Academy's Department of Behavioral Sciences and Leadership. The chair of this 40-person department was Colonel (now retired General) Gary Packard, a Ph.D. developmental psychologist who served in the Air Force for more than 30 years, including some time as the Commander of a Flying Training Squadron and a deployment as the Director of Staff of the Air Force's largest expeditionary wing. In some ways he is a stereotypical man: career military, fit, trained as a pilot, plays golf, drinks beer, and had won the department's fantasy football pool two years in a row. In other ways, he is not stereotypical at all: a developmental psychologist (a field quite dominated by women), emotionally warm with a deep caring for his subordinates, and the Air Force's lead writer on the Department of Defense study that led to the repeal of Don't Ask, Don't Tell Act in 2010, which now not only allows gay and lesbian service members to acknowledge their same-sex partnerships, but also allows them to gain military benefits, such as access to health insurance, for their spouses if they choose to marry.

Gary is an Alpha male. He loves to run things. He was a dominant figure at the Academy, but he is far from the bully we think of Alphas as being. He is more than capable of being forceful when he believes the situation calls for it, but I never saw him demean, threaten, or disrespect anyone, nor did I ever see him assert dominance for the mere sake of being dominant. He does not need to, because his authority is respected. Nearly everyone who works for him speaks of him with the utmost reverence, even dare I say, love. He is perhaps the most impressive leader I have ever met. I have also met Alphas who are bullies (whom I will not name): people (and not just men) who abuse their authority, intimidate and humiliate their subordinates, and dominate through making people fearful. Just for the sake of illustration I will refer to the composite of the bully Alpha as a guy named Biff after the bully in the *Back to the Future* films.

Now my apologies to Gary, but I am going to compare him to a monkey. Biff, I do not feel too badly about. As primatologist Frans de Waal (2005) points out, the stereotype of the Alpha is Biff, the animal who uses violence or the threat of it as a path to dominance. He beats others up as needed to maintain his position and is often seen engaging in what primatologists call the "bipedal swagger" in which he stands up straight and shifts from side to side, sometimes accompanied by chest beating depending on the species. This is a body language warning that says, "Get out of my way or you're going to be sorry," because he will rush and beat up whomever does not step aside.

Biffs exist in the primate world, but de Waal reports that they are in the minority for a very simple reason. The other animals do not like them and will form coalitions to overthrow them. The most successful Alphas are like Gary—de Waal calls them "populists." They lead the troop by ensuring fairness in, for instance, food sharing and breaking up fights, especially between juveniles, as the longer the conflict lasts, the more likely it is that the mothers will be fighting and further disrupting the troop. It is a little anthropomorphic, but de Waal describes the primate Gary as an animal that the others love, to the point where one populist maintained his Alpha position for the better part of two decades. No Biff could do that; as he aged, younger and stronger animals would take over. Too often, de Waal says, we think of survival of the fittest as being a matter of eliminating the unfit, but one can display fitness in many ways, for instance by being good at finding food, maintaining harmony within the troop, and ensuring that others do not get hurt.

Back to evolutionary theory. The gender evolutionary psychologists propose that the sexes take different pathways to adaptation because survival and reproductive success can mean different things to males and females. I am no theoretical biologist, but it appears that for physical characteristics, there is little dispute to this claim. But there is a wrinkle. As Richard Francis (2004) points out, if I develop a trait that makes me more adaptive, it is not necessarily encoded on the Y-chromosome, and therefore I would pass that characteristic on to my daughters as well as my sons because I have an X-chromosome that is inherited by both. Francis calls this process of intergenerational transmission across both sexes "intergender hitchhiking." Theoretically, it is not enough to demonstrate that a characteristic confers more of an advantage to one sex than the other; it must also be the case that there is a disadvantage for the other sex. He cites several examples.

Ornithologically speaking, one extensive difference between the avian and the human worlds in that in birds, males are usually a lot flashier than females. Standing out in one's brightly colored plumage turns out to be a real two-edged sword. Female birds show stronger attraction to more flamboyant males, so the cock-of-the-walk has more mating opportunities and thus a better chance to propagate his genes. On the other hand, he stands out like a sore thumb to predators, so his coloration also puts him at greater risk of being someone's lunch. For some reason which I will leave to the ornithologists to explain, brightly colored female birds do not seem to garner more allure than their blander counterparts. Thus, bright coloration on female birds confers on them none of the advantage and all of the disadvantages that this attribute affords males, creating a situation that leads to a "sex-dimorphic" characteristic. The sex of the cardinals that fly near my house is immediately obvious: the males are a bright crimson color, the females more of a dull brownish hue.

When two male moose, deer, or elk face off in mating competitions, the one with the smaller antlers backs down, which begs the question: how do they know? Maybe they look at their reflections in the streams? At any rate, antlers are strongly related to mating opportunities, although they come at a price. Antlers are rich in blood vessels and must be regrown every year, and so there is a great deal of calorie expenditure invested in the rack. Females do not need antlers and they are better off conserving calories to invest in the more important task of nourishing their progeny during pregnancy and the early life of their offspring. There are rare cases where cows grow antlers, but, in moose at least, it is because of a biological accident, a hormone imbalance. Again, females would incur none of the asset and all of the liability, and so antlers on cows of all species are more the exception than the rule.

When animals such as rhinoceros have horns instead of antlers, their existence on females is the opposite—more the rule than the exception. Horns grow from keratin, the same type of protein that makes up hair and nails. In contrast to antlers, horns are permanent and thus there is no seasonal calorie expenditure that could make for a disadvantage for females. Horns are thus relatively cheap and so the default is for the cows to have them.

This is the same reason that men have nipples—because they come at little evolutionary cost. The sexes are homologous, meaning that they grow from the same tissue. Prenatally, the default option is for the zygote to develop into a female unless acted upon by androgens, the masculinizing hormones. The structure called the genital tubercule develops into a clitoris if this hormone is not present or does not function; it develops into a penis when the hormone acts upon the fetus. (Sigmund Freud had it exactly backwards when he described the clitoris as a miniature penis—not surprising, as he is often cited for his phallocentricity. The penis is more accurately described as an enlarged clitoris.) In fact, there are people who have an X- and a Y-chromosome who did not respond prenatally to the masculinizing hormone and who thus look like females despite being genetically male, a condition called Androgen Insensitivity Syndrome.

As I discussed in Chapter 2, comedian Rob Becker had a remarkably successful stage show using the rubric of man the hunter and woman the gatherer. Although it is true that men in foraging societies tended to do more hunting than their female counterparts, there are wide cross-cultural variations. In some societies, there was a rather strict gendered division of labor with men being the exclusive hunters and women the exclusive gatherers, but in others, both sexes did both activities. Nobody has found a society where women are the exclusive hunters, probably because pregnancy and breast-feeding compromise their mobility and men's upper-body strength could have been a hunting asset before the advent of modern weapons, depending on what was being hunted. Some evolutionary psychologists claim that males' advantage in spatial skills evolved as a hunting asset, conveniently leaving out cultural variations like Chinese girls outperforming American boys in spatial skills. Some theorists even propose that men's unwillingness to ask for directions arises from their reluctance to display less-than-optimal spatial skills and thus communicate that their genes are not the best (Francis, 2004). But it would seem to me that spatial skills are also a gathering asset—remembering where to find the food. And as Francis points out, even if spatial awareness confers a survival/reproductive advantage to males, it would confer no corresponding disadvantage to females. There is no downside to having a good sense of direction. It is not enough to say it's good for the gander; it must be bad for the goose as well.

Barbara Ehrenreich (1983) speculated that hunting may not have been as deeply engrained millions of years ago as it was in more recent history. Think about it: do you think a group of Fred Flintstones could bring down a 6-ton wooly mammoth with a bunch of sharpened sticks? Perhaps, Ehrenreich says, our brains evolved during a long period when we were less often the hunt*ers* and more often the hunt*ed*. She argues that meat consumption during the Paleolithic period was more often from scavenging than from hunting, and that therefore the activity of hunting developed too late to have made its way into our brain structures through the snail's pace of evolution.

Following is a story from my life that well illustrates that biological forces do not work in isolation, especially for humans. In October of 1986, I ran my first and only marathon in Richmond, Virginia. I trained for 12 weeks with my then-roommate and later co-author John Lynch. To be allowed into the race, one must sign a form that says you agree to stop if in the judgment of race officials, your health is in danger. Although I trained thoroughly, I had no experience running that distance and I made the mistake of starting out a little too fast. As a result, by the second half of the race I noticed that every time I passed one of the National Guard soldiers who were stationed around the route, they picked up their radio. I imagined their saying, "Yeah, contacting four-oh-niner. Yeah, number 444. Yeah, he's gonna die any second." But I made it to the end by walking most of the last seven miles on very wobbly legs, and fortunately the last 100 yards of the race was downhill so I could run through the finish line merely by leaning forward and thus not look as badly as I felt to the crowd gathered there. When I crossed the line, two people grabbed me by the arms and passed me off to a third person whom one of them told, "we're watching him." I vaguely recall someone asking if I was okay and my telling them that I was despite not being an authority on the subject at the time. My biology was screaming for me to stop and lie down somewhere, but I had spent 12 weeks preparing for this day and I was hell-bent on finishing. I still remember my time: 3:53:41.1. Not bad for a guy who is decidedly not built like a distance runner.

Look at the considerable examples of how situational or learning factors lead one to override one's biological instincts. Athletic training often entails remarkable suffering, but athletes undergo it because they are committed to the outcome. If a huge man is running right at you at full speed, your biology tells you to get out of the way. But if you are a middle linebacker you do the opposite because you have learned to do so. In 2013, 64-year old Diana Nyad swam 110 miles from Havana, Cuba to Key West, Florida (a feat no man has accomplished) in 52 hours, 53 minutes. In 1965, high school student Randy Gardner went 264 hours—11 days—without sleeping! I am guessing that Nyad's biology was telling her to stop and Gardner's was telling him to get some sleep. Anorexics starve their bodies because they have bought into a cultural myth that skinny is good. And in the fall of 2013, I watched first-year students at the Air Force Academy undergo extremes in military physical challenges to claim their place in the Cadet Wing.

Biology makes a difference, but it is anything but destiny. As we have seen, the evidence that men are hardwired differently from women is scant at best and largely unprovable, and that in nearly every case, the ability of environment, social influence, learning, and will can dwarf the effects of many biological forces. In guest lectures at colleges and universities, audience members often ask, "but aren't men and women fundamentally different because of our biologies?" As we have seen, not so much. But although this is an important question for social scientists, the more important question for the rest of us is, "how do you want to live your life?" Do you want to make decisions based on your goals and values or merely go along with the program?

# 4

# MIRRORS OF THE SOUL

## The fiction that appearance is reality

I do not know who coined the aphorism "appearance is reality" but it is a remarkable favorite among motivational speakers and those who train business people and military personnel. I understand that it is a catchphrase to remind people that they need to manage others' impressions of them to be successful, but I really loathe the saying because, as a psychologist, my job is to look for what is beneath the surface. Appearance is appearance. We can only guess at someone's inner reality from their outward appearance unless we expend time and effort in learning how they experience the world and what they value. From the beginning of our graduate training, counseling and clinical psychologists (and social workers, pastoral counselors, and others in the helping professions) hone the skills of gaining a deep understanding of another's experience that goes far beyond observations of the external.

My friend and colleague Ryan is a young psychologist on the faculty of a mid-sized university. Several years ago, I had the pleasure of co-presenting a workshop on how to teach the Psychology of Men at the annual convention of the American Psychological Association. Ryan began his portion of the workshop with a story that I found particularly memorable because it provides an excellent gendered example of the discrepancy between appearance and reality. Like me, Ryan has remained in contact with a select group of friends from his college years and reunites with them from time to time. Perhaps owing to the fact that he is considerably younger, his group is larger than my foursome: thirteen good friends, all of them men, get together for a long weekend every few years to reminisce, catch up, and have some fun.

For a lot of people, summer weekends while they are in their twenties seem like an endless stream of bachelor/bachelorette parties and weddings. Ryan was the first of his group to marry at age 24, and so he and his best man arranged a four-day reunion cruise for all the friends on a houseboat in the Illinois River. Ryan had a secret agenda: if they were in the middle of the river, it would be impossible for someone to drag him to a strip club, which is, of course, an all-too-frequent standard activity for a bachelor party.

Men are all different. Some like to go and watch women take off their clothes. Others like Ryan and I do not. We find it demeaning to both the patrons and performers. One childhood memory stuck out for Ryan. His father was a salesman whom he greatly admired and hoped to emulate. Although his father never told him that he should stay away from strip clubs, Ryan recalls that the other salesmen often went to them, especially after they had closed a big deal. He also remembers that his father never joined in. He told Ryan, "We finalized a big contract yesterday after weeks and weeks of work. They went to the strip club and I went home."

Both Ryan and I had similar experiences in college: dating a feminist-identified woman and listening to her experience. For me it was a woman named Ginny with whom I was wildly infatuated. I still recall this exchange from so many years ago:

CHRIS: Some of the girls in my class are working on this project …
GINNY: Girls? You have children in your class?
CHRIS: No, you know what I mean, college girls.
GINNY: They're not girls; you should call them women.
CHRIS: What the hell difference does that make? You know who I'm talking about.
GINNY: Yeah, you're talking about a group of people you don't respect enough to refer to as adults.

That lesson has stayed with me my entire life and I am on a decades-long, albeit not very successful campaign to have college students refer to adult females as women, since "guy" and "girl" are not equivalent terms, and few people would refer to an adult man as a boy.

I realize that I just dropped the F-word: feminist, which sets some people off because they have a distorted view that feminists are man-hating, freeze-the-sperm-and-kill-'em-all crazies, and yet women who identify as feminists score lower, not higher, on scales measuring hostility toward men (Rudman & Fairchild, 2007). Feminists are all different, of course, but we should remember that about 90% of feminists are married to men and that many have sons whom they love. Feminists as a group actually hold higher opinions of men than non-feminists (Anderson, Kanner, & Elsayegh, 2009). They believe that most men can be trusted and that most are decent human beings. As Charis Kramarae and Paula Treichler (1986) famously defined it, "Feminism is the radical notion that women are people," and I have never seen a feminist group platform that includes statements about antipathy toward men.

I attended a family member's wedding a few years back and the minister was very socially conservative. He got to the place in the ceremony where the bride takes her vows and said, "Now—this is the part of the ceremony where we say that the wife should obey her husband and the feminists don't much like that. Maybe that's why the feminists don't have husbands." To the contrary, men married to feminist-identified women reported greater stability in their relationship and greater sexual satisfaction than men paired with non-feminists. And women in relationships with men who hold feminist beliefs reported similar benefits (Rudman & Phelan, 2007).

So, if women are people and we think of them as such, then it is uncomfortable to go to a place where they are little more than naked objects to be leered at. I was dragged to strip clubs as a young man and found them to have an atmosphere of aggression, which was disconcerting, and to be demeaning of both women and men—of women as valued only for their sexuality and of men as needing to pay to have women pretend that they are sexually attracted to them. Call me sentimental, but for me the best thing about sex is to be desired, and paying someone to pretend she desires me? I can't make the whole trip. And as anti-pornography activist Gail Dines (2013) said, "To be unclothed in the presence of the clothed is to be powerless." I wonder how many men would be willing to be naked and sit with a group of fully clothed people.

Ryan's plan to avoid the strip club worked perfectly the first of the four nights, but he had forgotten that the boat had to be docked every evening to keep it from running into something, and on the second night, they put ashore in what he described as "middle of nowhere Illinois." As fate would have it, through the magic of the Internet, one of the men discovered that this little town had a "gentlemen's club," which to me is an amazing euphemism, like calling the MX Missile the "Peacekeeper." What gentleman would ogle and objectify women?

Predictably, one of the men announced, "They have a strip club here and we're going!" A couple of others joined in with enthusiasm. Ryan looked around and nobody else seemed as reluctant as he felt (note the discrepancy between Ryan's rather neutral appearance and his internal reality). He wanted everybody to have fun and did not want to be the "wet blanket," and so he went along. As guest of honor, he made it clear that he wanted no lap dances and definitely no back room visits, and his friends were willing to agree to those limits. They paid a man to drive them to the club, piling in the back of a pickup truck (which is another moment of especially poor judgment, but fortunately they arrived at the club and made it back to the boat without consequence). Ryan spent his time at the club as a sort of informal anthropologist, talking with the strippers as people and learning about what it was like to do what they do. He later admitted that he had fun, although it was not exactly the kind of fun some of his friends had. If it is fun to talk to people and understand their experiences, you may be destined to become a psychologist, although Ryan did not know it at the time.

Fast forward to a few years later and the next bachelor party. All of the same men were in attendance and once again, one of them announced that there would be a strip club trip. This time Ryan found his voice and told his friends that he did not want to go. Another friend, empowered by Ryan's courage, joined him in dissent, but they were told, "Shut up; it's not about you. It's about the groom." And the two men again allowed themselves to be dragged there. This time Ryan and the other dissenter sat in the back, shared a pitcher of beer, did not watch the show and complained about the others. Ryan described them as talking "like the two grumpy old men from The Muppets."

The Decade of Weddings was far from over, and not surprisingly, Ryan found himself in the strip club dilemma a third time just a few years later. In the time since the previous reunion, Ryan had gone through some changes. He had left his job in business to go to graduate school to train to become a psychotherapist and was developing an interest in the psychology of men and masculinity along with acquiring the skills to look beneath the surface. And one of his psychotherapy clients worked as a stripper. She had remarkable disdain for the male customers and hated the feeling that she got when they leered at her, and yet she needed money so desperately that she continued in the job. She said that she would quit in a heartbeat if she could find another way to make ends meet. She had symptoms of anxiety and depression and although she did not connect them to her work, Ryan did. Moreover, Ryan and his wife had recently given birth to a baby girl. He could easily imagine how badly he would feel about her becoming a stripper when she grew up.

Ryan was no longer satisfied with going along to the club and silently resisting; he did not want to participate in any way. As he later told me, he had decided, "I got to the point where I could never do this again and live with myself regardless of how much pressure they put on me." He told his friends adamantly that he would not go under any circumstances, that he had a big problem with strip clubs, and that they should be more aware of the sexism in which they were participating.

Then a remarkable social moment took place. The men had a serious and somewhat heated discussion about the morality of strip clubs. What emerged from this discussion was surprising to all: 9 of the 13 men did *not* like strip clubs and did not want to go. Like Ryan, the majority had believed that everyone else liked the activity (this is a phenomenon known as *pluralistic ignorance*). The other four men, now identified as clearly in the minority, nevertheless went by themselves to ogle naked women, but now that conformity had been broken, the other 9 stayed at the rental house and enjoyed food, drinks, and conversation. And the "tradition" of watching women take off their clothes as a part of the reunion died immediately. The four men in the minority had believed that their attitudes were normative when, in fact, they were not, a phenomenon called *false consensus*.

The Appearance is Reality fiction is the tendency to assume that people's behavior corresponds exactly with their inner experience (e.g., the belief that a person who shows no outward emotional *response* to a situation must not be having an emotional *experience*). But behavior does not always reflect personality. Most men do not believe that they fit the cultural stereotype of masculinity ("I'm different from most guys") because they tend to compare their internal experience with other men's social performances (Kilmartin et al., 2008).

In the past 20 years or so, a line of research known as *social norms marketing* has emerged. Mostly aimed at college students, the approach is based on the theory that students have distorted views about what most of their peers are like, and as a result, they sometimes behave in unhealthy ways to fit in. The early work in this area was around the issue of binge drinking. It might surprise you to find out that most college students who drink alcohol do so moderately and responsibly. This fact flies directly in the face of the widely held stereotype that college students are a bunch of drunks. Do not get me wrong; there is an awful lot of drinking going on at nearly every campus in the United States, but the student who gets falling-down drunk every weekend—we'll call him Al K. Holboy—is more the exception than the rule. It is easy to see why people think Al K. is the typical college student. If you go to a student party, whom are you going to notice, remember, and talk about the next day? Mo Deration, who has three beers and pleasant conversation in the kitchen over the course of several hours, or Al K., who chugs four beer bongs in 20 minutes and throws up all over himself? It is difficult to notice what people are *not* doing.

The social norms marketing approach is to gather data about the actual behavior of students through careful survey techniques and then to publicize the information about what most people actually do. The publicity takes the form of posters, ads in campus newspapers, and spots on campus radio or television stations saying, "MOST students at Wattsamatta U. have 0–4 drinks when they party." The messages are descriptive, not prescriptive. You do not say, "Hey, don't drink so much!" You merely tell students what most others do. When done well, these public information campaign efforts have been effective in reducing binge drinking on many campuses (Berkowitz, 2004).

More than a decade ago, I became interested in whether the social norms approach could be used to reduce the perception that the typical man is a sexist pig. Most men like and respect women and are bothered when other men call women by animal names or the names of their genitals, tell demeaning jokes, or worst of all, suggest that rape is normal and acceptable. But they overestimate other men's comfort with this bigotry. It is like laughing at a joke you do not think is funny. We have all done it, and if I watched you laugh at that joke, wouldn't it be reasonable for me to assume that you liked it? The only way I would know that you did not is if you let me in on your private reaction.

This is what I did together with a team of student researchers: we gave men surveys measuring sexism, rape-supportive attitudes, and levels of comfort–discomfort with other men's sexism. The latter survey described situations that might take place within a group of men, such as the following: you have been talking to a woman at a party. When she goes to get another glass of punch, your male roommate says to you, "That punch is so strong. Keep her drinking; you'll be guaranteed to get laid," which suggests that it is permissible to try to get a woman drunk for purposes of sexual access. Then we asked them to indicate how comfortable they were with hearing this statement on a scale from 1 ("very comfortable") to 7 ("very uncomfortable"). All these surveys were anonymous. As is often done by researchers, we had each participant generate a code made up of the last four digits of his cell phone number and the month in which he was born. That way, we could match up the various surveys without associating any of them with any specific person. This procedure reduces the likelihood that someone would lie so he could look good to us and also protects the privacy of the participants.

After collecting the surveys on these attitudes, we gave them the same surveys again, but this time with different instructions: think of a fellow male student on this campus whom you know well and complete the surveys the way you think he would fill them out. Amusingly, one student asked, "How am *I* supposed to *know* what my friend *thinks?*" Clearly, he had no experience with conversations with his closest friends about their attitudes and values.

We collected these and asked them to do the three surveys once more, this time estimating the attitudes of "the average male student on this campus." To summarize: we collected data on Self, Friend, and Typical Guy and divided the scores by the number of participants to describe the averages in each category. We were comparing the *actual*, or more accurately, *reported* average (Self) with the *perceived* averages (Friend and Typical Guy) (Carr et al., 2002). We believed that the participants were being honest in their self-reports (having little motivation to lie on anonymous surveys) although one could challenge that assumption.

The findings of this first phase of the experiment were not surprising. There was a significant difference between Self ratings and both Friend and Typical Guy ratings. Most college men see themselves as having rather low levels of sexism, rape-supportive attitudes, and comfort with other men's sexism, but they also believe that they are rather unusual in that regard. The difference between the actual and perceived average was so large that our statistical tests indicated that this finding could be expected by chance alone less than one time out of a thousand. There was no statistically significant difference between the Friend and Typical Guy averages. The bottom line of this step in the research was that men were saying, "I'm not sexist, but my friends are, and most guys are."

Armed with these findings, we were ready to take the next step and publicize the norms to the college community. We placed half-page ads in the school newspaper and put posters in prominent places on the campus with messages like, "80% of Mary Washington men think it's wrong to make jokes that demean women." Our committee on "community values and behavioral expectations," whose job it is to do what they can to make the campus a healthy and respectful place, gave us an internal grant to finance the project.

The newspaper ads were very noticeable, but it is hard to get people's attention with posters; anyone who has ever been on a campus will tell you that every bulletin board is teeming with paper. However, in my years of working there, I had noticed that there are very underutilized advertising spaces: classrooms. Generally, when someone wants to put up posters on a campus to advertise an event, sell something, or promote a cause, they take their ads and a stapler and go around to every bulletin board they can find in an hour's time. You cannot do this in a classroom on an instructional day because classes are being held (unless you are willing to really violate a social norm by entering the room in the middle of class). My team waited until 9:50 a.m. and put posters in every classroom they could for the ten minute between-class interval, and then did the same at the next hour and the next until our message found a captive audience in pretty much every classroom on campus. It might not surprise you to know that students are not always exactly singularly focused on the instruction and often will look around the room during class.

This was cool stuff, for research geeks anyway. We were trying to alter the perception of an attitude with an environmental intervention. And it worked—to an extent. When we brought in our research participants three weeks later and asked them to do the same surveys, their Self ratings did not change (we did not expect them to, as our information campaign was focused on how they perceive other men), but their perception of Typical Guy sexism became remarkably more accurate, still higher than their Self ratings but not significantly so (Carr et al., 2002).

But this is what we did not expect: their ratings of "a man on this campus whom you know well" did not budge at all! Before the information campaign, they were saying "I'm not sexist, but my friends are, and most guys are." Three weeks later, they were saying, "I'm not sexist and I've learned that most guys aren't either, but my friends are still sexist pigs." It was not until this point that I realized what we had neglected in our information campaign: it was all focused on Typical Guy, and we mistakenly assumed that they would see their friends as typical. But "the average male student on this campus" is an abstraction; your friend is a real person. This was a huge problem because our ultimate goal was to get men to speak up like Ryan at the strip club suggestion when they hear something offensive. They are not likely to do that if they do not think there are some like-minded men in the room (more on this later). So, we had to design another study to handle the issue.

The goal of the next study was to get men to look into the faces of the peers they underestimated. We used the same procedure and surveys, but only two this time. In groups of 8 to 12, they first filled out the measures to describe their own attitudes, and then we gave them the same measures and asked them to complete them as they thought the "average man in the room" would respond. Again, the discrepancy between the real average and the perceived average was enormous. This time, my then-student Mike Kuchler delivered the social norms intervention in real time. Mike is a pretty masculine looking man—athletic build and fairly tall, and he has a tattoo of barbed wire encircling one of his biceps, although I cannot recall if it was visible for this experiment. He is also a very gentle man whom other men seem to not find intimidating, so he was perfect for delivering the intervention. He explained how people misjudge others by comparing their inner experiences with others' appearances, again using the example of laughing at a joke you do not think is funny. Then, using bar graphs, he showed them the results of their group's real vs. perceived averages. In the control group, we merely gave them the surveys and sent them home. We brought both groups back three weeks later and found that we largely had corrected the overestimation of peers' sexism, rape supportive attitudes, and comfort with other men's sexism in the intervention group. The control group, as expected, did not change. The bottom line is that it is important to look into the faces of the men you are misjudging rather than to merely understand your error in the abstract (Kilmartin et al., 2008).

One important caveat: we tried to do long-term follow-up and were unable to get enough participants to measure whether the effect had endured, and we know from other studies that attitude changes frequently rebound. Therefore, I am not suggesting that a brief intervention like this changes people forever. In fact, it probably takes frequent doses of the message along with other techniques to bring a durable change. I would very much like to see other researchers extend this work.

Indulge me while I go back to the classic social psychology research from the 1960s that underlies this approach. Social psychologist Solomon Asch (1965) and his colleagues brought people into their lab and told them that they were doing an experiment on visual perception. They showed them a vertical line and asked them to say which of three comparison vertical lines was closest in length to the original line. They said they would just go around the room and ask each person in turn. Put yourself in the participant's place; you are at the end of the line and will give your opinion after nine others. You look at the lines; it is not a difficult task. Line C is obviously the correct answer. The first person answers "Line B," which is unquestionably incorrect. "Well," you think, "maybe something is wrong with their eyes." The second person also says "Line B." What a coincidence! Two people with bad eyes in the same room! The third person says "Line B," followed by the fourth and the fifth giving the same answer. Now you are beginning to think that you might be the one with the bad eyes.

What is going on here? The key is the researcher's subfield of psychology. I have a rather cynical synonym for social psychologist: Liar. These researchers are notorious for deceiving their participants by first telling them they are studying one thing when they are investigating something else and second, with the use of confederates, who are actors following a script. In this case, you are the only "naïve participant" in the room and all the others are giving wrong answers on a schedule. They are not studying visual perception; they are studying conformity—unspoken social pressure to behave like other members within a group. The grand question: what are the factors that determine whether or not a person will give an obviously incorrect answer due to social pressure exerted by others, even if the others are strangers?

The control condition is one in which there is no social pressure at all—when you are just doing the line-judging task on your own. In this case, people give the correct answer nearly 100% of the time. As I said, it is not a difficult task. But when everyone else in the room gives the incorrect answer, the naïve participant goes along with it as often as 50% or more of the time, a very strong conformity effect.

The most interesting finding for me is that if just one of the confederates gives the correct answer, conformity drops sharply, from around 50 percent to around 20 percent. Asch called the strong level of conformity when one is alone against the majority the *unanimity effect*. But once the researchers directed just a single confederate to refuse to conform, they demonstrated that there is a huge difference between being one against nine and being two against eight. Even in a small minority, a single ally can empower someone to speak up. Going back to Ryan and the strip club friends, at first Ryan thought he was alone against the entire group. Once he understood that he had a single ally to support him, he spoke up and gained some traction, and by the third time, the two of them pretty much led a revolt and discovered that they were actually in a strong majority.

This is what we were trying to do in our social norms study: to increase the perception of the ally. In his book on the extended adolescence of the American male, *Guyland*, Michael Kimmel (2008) relates a story about a similar process taking place with fraternity men. The campus Kimmel describes is not atypical; the fraternity houses on one end and the sororities on the other. Interestingly, often sororities are forbidden by their charters to throw parties, perhaps an antiquated rule going back to a time when throwing a party where one served alcohol was considered unladylike. All the parties take place at the fraternity houses, and it was not uncommon for a few women to spend the night at the fraternity house with a boyfriend or hook-up. The following morning, the women would walk home across the campus.

My university does not have a Greek system, nor does the Air Force Academy where I taught for a year, nor does the Naval Academy, where I did an extensive consultation, but in all three places, nearly all the students know what the common term is for women making their way back to the dormitory or sorority house in the morning: the *Walk of Shame*. I have always been amazed that we, as heterosexual men, want women to have sex with us, and then we denigrate them for doing it.

One group of fraternity pledges were required to gather on the porch of their house on weekend mornings to jeer at the women who were taking the Walk of Shame. On his visit there, Kimmel asked the men privately how they felt about doing so. Many said that it made them uncomfortable, that some of these women were friends, and that this activity did not do much for the fraternity's reputation. Michael asked, "Then why do you do it?" and the answer was that everyone else seemed okay with it. The question "Is everyone else okay with it?" is an empirical one, and Kimmel encouraged the men to gather some informal data to answer it by suggesting to individual men that the next time they found themselves on the porch, that they might look around to see if they can find another man who by his body language appears that he might be uncomfortable like they are. Then as soon as the opportunity presents itself, pull him aside and have a private conversation about whether or not he really enjoys jeering at these women. When the men began to do this, they discovered that very few of them enjoyed this activity—again much like Ryan's strip club discovery—and so they called a chapter meeting to discuss the issue. When Kimmel returned a couple of months later, they had stopped the morning jeering at women. A simple intervention changed an organization just by providing basic information about how most men really are—a small but important change in the fraternity's culture.

People toss around the term "peer pressure" a lot, and it is almost always used to describe the social influences on people to do things that are harmful. But social pressure can be positive and as we have found, the good men are in the majority. The problem is that they often do not know that they are, and thus their voices are effectively silenced. Once they learn that they can speak up and be supported by other men, and once they learn the skill of challenging others who behave in sexist ways, they can be remarkably effective in producing cultural change. Why would someone invest time and effort in learning this skill? When he decides that it is important, just as he might spend hours becoming better at basketball, fishing, carpentry, writing, or playing a musical instrument.

And what I often tell men is that you do not have to get out your flip chart and make a 40-minute presentation ("I attended Dr. Kilmartin's seminar on masculinity; let me explain to you how sexism operates …"). A well-placed phrase indicating your disapproval can be remarkably powerful. In response to "Let's go to the strip club," you can say, "No thanks. I don't want that to be part of my life." Some other great phrases: "Hey! Have some respect for the woman," "Yeah, I'm sure your girlfriend or mother would love to hear you say that," or simply, "I don't like the way you talk about women; it bothers me." Or if you are bothered and cannot muster an articulate response, just get the guy to repeat the comment. "I'm sorry; what did you say?" Now he has to say it very consciously instead of just spouting off without thinking (Kilmartin, 2017).

> When you yelled "nice ass" at me from down the street, I thought that maybe you might be attracted to me and I wondered if you'd like to go have a drink sometime.
>
> *Said: No Woman Ever.*

Street harassment is not about sex; it is about intimidation. Men do not behave in sexist ways to win women's approval. Do you think that a woman doing the Walk of Shame would want to date or hook up with the guy who jeered at her? Men behave in sexist ways to win the approval of other men. So, it is obvious when it will stop: when the good guys in the majority amplify their voices and let these men know that they do not like it, and thus the badly behaving men lose instead of gain status for their actions. I discuss this process further in Chapter 6.

At the Air Force Academy, I was invited to do a presentation on sexism and sexual assault to all the academic department heads. This was an exciting opportunity, as people in power have the ability to set the tone within their individual cultures. I helped them to understand the issue and encouraged them to do what they can to create a fully respectful work and teaching environment. During a break, one of the department heads told me what I found to be a remarkable story.

He said that once when he was in college, he went to a bar and grill with two of his friends for drinks and brunch. They arrived rather early, and so the restaurant was largely empty when a family came in—appearing to be parents visiting their daughter at college and accompanied by her high school aged sister. The men found the daughters to be attractive. He and one of his friends began to make loud, sexualized comments, quite audible in this largely empty restaurant. He said that at one point, one of the women looked over at him and he realized in retrospect that she appeared to be uncomfortable. "We were being jerks," as he put it. After a couple of these remarks, the third man who was not making comments looked at his two good friends and in a disgusted and emphatic tone, simply said "SHUT UP!"

The storyteller told me that, in that moment, he felt remarkably ashamed. In fact, the two of them did shut up, and he spent a lot of time thinking about what had gotten into him that he thought that he was entitled to behave that way. The most important part of the story was that this man, now in his mid-40s, said "that lesson has stayed with me for my entire life," just as my college conversation with Ginny, about referring to adult women as "girls" had. Two words from a valued friend changed him forever and he never again harassed a woman. He also learned how to challenge others who acted disrespectfully. That is the power of the healthy voice when it is amplified, and one small step toward associating men with dignity and respect.

Because many men have not thought about or been taught about the social pressure of masculinity, they enact these performances and fail to examine what parts of themselves they are hiding from other men, sometimes leaving them with a vague sense of discomfort and feeling like they are different from other men in some important ways, as they compare their inner experiences with other men's appearances. And so, these caring and respectful aspects of self are—I use this term very intentionally—*closeted*, meaning that they are hiding parts of the self to avoid the anticipated disapproval of others.

Men are told to perform masculinity in so many unnecessary places: in how we talk and move, in what we are interested in, what colors we like, how we cross our legs, what we like to eat and drink, and the list goes on and on. For some reason that is unclear to me, when I walk into a bar, I am only supposed to drink things that are brown: beer, scotch, or whiskey. Never a Cape Cod or, God forbid, a cosmopolitan (we know what color *those* are!).

Every semester during my 30-year teaching career, I assigned my students the task of interviewing a man about his gendering: what his early role models were, how he learned about what it means to be a man, what kinds of behaviors he avoids and embraces, etc. They can interview anyone they want, as long as he is an adult, and as long as he is not a boyfriend, husband, or partner (I have found that these papers are terrible, because the student writes about just how wonderful he is and finds it difficult or impossible to be critical). Students have interviewed strangers, brothers, fathers, grandfathers, and friends of a variety of ages, occupations, sexualities, and masculinities. In the aggregate, these interviews demonstrate what few people seem to know—that men are all different. The thing that we share is the social pressure to behave and experience ourselves in ways that the culture defines as appropriate for the bodies we are perceived as inhabiting. But what differentiates us is that individual men's responses to this pressure are widely variable. As I wrote earlier, we all know men who appear to be walking stereotypes, but we also all know those who love children, do not like sports, enjoy the company of women, and discuss how they feel.

I have found that many, although certainly not all, of the middle-aged and older men interviewed are somewhat aware of the gender pressure they experience and "pick their spots" to conform and to resist. Many, although certainly not all, of the younger men report feeling a little straitjacketed by masculine norms and a little helpless to resist them. The message I hear again and again from these men is "I can't be myself around my friends," and yet they rarely say why. But, it is clear that they have a vague sense that they would not be accepted if they revealed certain parts of themselves. Because nobody is helping them name the social pressure, they feel powerless to resist it.

My favorite assignment from my Psychology of Men class is what I call the "wide open journal." Students can write about anything from their everyday lives that has anything to do with gender: an article they read, movie they saw, conversation they engaged in, behavior they observed, or thoughts that occurred to them. The goal is to get them to notice gendered arrangements in their everyday lives and think critically about them, and the assignment is at once the simplest and the most effective one I have ever used. They become both excited and not just a little annoyed at what they are learning. One student even said to me, "Thanks a lot. I can't even watch television anymore." At that point I pull out my favorite quote from Thomas, Cardinal Wolsey (1471–1530), "Be very, very careful what you put into that head, because you will never, ever get it out." There are both advantages and disadvantages to becoming gender aware. If there were nothing but advantages, everyone would be doing it; if there were nothing but disadvantages, nobody would be doing it. Of course, I strongly believe that the upside far outweighs the downside, but I understand that some people would just prefer to watch the romantic comedy and not read too much into it.

I see a lot of gendered performances in my students' observations. One man asked his female friend to teach him how to knit but to please not tell his friends. Another confessed how much he likes sweet cocktails like cosmopolitans, pina coladas, wine coolers, and fuzzy navels, but that he only drinks these at home or when he is not in the company of other men. A third spoke of getting caught in the pouring rain and allowing himself to be absolutely soaked because he did not feel comfortable sharing an umbrella with his male friend. He was sure that if it were his girlfriend or another woman it would have been okay, but rather than understand that this avoidance made no real sense at all, his response was, "That's just the way it is. Men don't share umbrellas. Period."

There have actually been a couple of books published recently for men who want to learn feminine-defined skills but still retain stereotypical masculinity—one on knitting called *Knitting with Balls* and another on cooking called *Eat What You Want and Die Like a Man: The World's Unhealthiest Cookbook*. If you go to a hardware store, you may see men purchasing outdoor grills, pressure washers, and shop vacuums, which tells you that even traditionally-gendered men will cook, clean, and vacuum if those activities are defined as masculine. And during my year at the Air Force Academy, I learned that they had changed the name of the counseling center to the Peak Performance Center so that stereotypically masculine men and women could go for psychological help but retain their prejudice against those who struggle with mental health concerns.

One of the most revealing and heartrending student journal stories came from one of my Austrian students, Melanie, whom I taught when I was a Fulbright Scholar at the University of Klagenfurt in 2007. Melanie had a part-time job as a bartender, and one afternoon around 4:00, one of her regulars, Markus, comes in, sits at the bar, and orders a beer. There is barely anyone in the bar at this time, and so she is not very busy. She notices that something about him does not look quite right and asks him if there is something bothering him. Markus tells Melanie that his girlfriend of three years has just "dumped" him. He had thought that they were on the path to marriage, and so he is devastated. He begins to cry as he tells her the story. Melanie listens with a sympathetic ear and offers support.

A few minutes later, she glances to her right and sees a small group of men entering the bar, which she recognizes as Markus's friends. Immediately Markus jumps up from the bar and calls out, (Melanie is translating here, and English is not her first language.) "Hey, my guys! That fucking bitch has left me! Come on let's drink and celebrate my returned freedom!" Melanie watches in amazement as the men order tequila shots (rather unusual for Europeans) and encourage Markus to approach women in the bar. After a couple of hours, they leave, and Markus returns to the bar, has one more beer, and starts crying again. Melanie's account was an incredible illustration of how pressured men feel to perform the stereotype, especially in the company of other men, by keeping their emotional and relational lives closeted.

The culture is replete with messages to men suggesting that they must conform to arbitrary definitions of masculinity. If ordinary men are comparing themselves with larger-than-life masculine images: professional athletes, body builders, astronauts, performers, and billionaires, then they are destined to feel like they do not measure up. And if I want to exploit this vague sense of inadequacy, I can use it to sell you something. The way the game is played is to send a subtle or not-so-subtle message that there is something wrong with you, but that you will be restored to your masculine self-esteem simply by purchasing the product. If you cannot be critical of the messages, you are very vulnerable to manipulation.

Beer companies are among the worst offenders. Miller Lite beer ran an entire series of "Man Law" commercials featuring a group of men, led by actor Burt Reynolds, seated around a conference table making decisions about how men should behave, such as refusing to put fruit in their beer or to touch the necks of their beer bottles together when toasting, instead clinking the bottoms, since if they clink together the spot on the bottle where their lips have been, "it's technically a kiss"—clearly a homophobic reference. And, of course, fruit in a beer is associated with Miller's competitors, Corona and Modelo, so it is no accident that they want to portray squeezing a lime into your beer as unmanly.

Miller also launched a series of commercials featuring men behaving in feminine ways such as wearing "skinny jeans" or carrying a bag that others refer to as a purse. The men who violate the masculine performance rules in these ads do not seem to care whether or not they drink a Miller or some other beer, thus they are portrayed as unmasculine because they cannot tell which is the best beer. In one of the most frequently aired ads, the strikingly attractive female bartender tells the man that when he starts to care what beer tastes like, "put down your purse and I'll give you a Miller Lite." The hypermasculine voiceover exhorts the listener to "man up" and order a Miller, thus threatening to unsex men who use the wrong product.

Perhaps the most over-the-top series of beer ads is the Dos Equis commercials featuring actor Jonathan Goldsmith as "the most interesting man in the world." Rather than featuring 20-something men as Miller and Budweiser do, Dos Equis uses an actor in his 70s, but he is quite masculine, albeit in a more sophisticated way than one sees in most beer ads. The Most Interesting Man in the World is absolutely sure of himself ("He once had an awkward moment, just to see what it feels like;" "He lives vicariously … through himself"); powerful ("His reputation precedes him the way that lightening precedes thunder"), and surrounded by beautiful and fawning young women. Goldsmith's tag line at the end of each commercial: "I don't always drink beer, but when I do, I prefer Dos Equis. Stay thirsty, my friend."

Nothing is an accident in advertising; every image is meticulously manipulated. What Dos Equis hopes is that you will watch the Most Interesting Man in the World and compare yourself with him, which will result in the unmistakable conclusion that you fall short of expectations in pretty much every way. But if you purchase the beer, maybe you will be more interesting, i.e., more masculine and sexually desirable. In most beer commercials, beer is presented as a proxy for men's friendships, associated with sexual access (just take a look at what women are doing in most of these ads, and they are almost exclusively attractive, thin, young, white women unless presented as comedic characters), and/or connected with outdoor activities, despite the fact that if you were doing these while drinking, it would be rather dangerous, and, as in a recent Bud Light campaign, also associated with being a good football fan. Nobody ever gets drunk or pays for a beer. They are not selling beer; they are selling a hypertrophied and stereotypical version of masculinity.

I confess that I do not drink much beer (I know—I've just relinquished my "man card"), preferring mixed drinks and (gasp!) wine. But I have certainly noticed men, especially young men, and how so many are so attached to their brand of beer. If he orders a Bud Light and the bartender says they are out of that brand, he becomes very unhappy because he does not like Miller Lite or Coors

Light. I have even seen men leave the bar because they could not get "their" brand.

In these moments I return to my undergraduate days and my first research experiment as a senior psychology major. Even back then I was a little mystified by the level of emotional attachment people, mainly men, had to their beer brands, even to the point of arguing with others about which was the "best" beer, and I began to wonder, first, who cares?, and second, can people even tell the difference? So, I set up a simple experiment. I had people stop by my residence hall room and drink from four shot glasses, each with a different and unlabeled beer, and tell me which one tasted best to them. I recorded their choices and had them come back the next evening to taste the same four beers in different order, again reporting their preferences. How many people picked the same beer twice? Twenty-five percent—exactly what would be expected by chance alone.

I was not surprised at the outcome because before one runs an experiment, the first task is to accomplish a review of the literature. What other studies have been run, with what methodologies? What do the results of these various studies tell us? This was well before the days of computer data bases and search engines. I had to sit in the library and page through whatever journals were available. But even with such primitive technology, I was astounded at how much I found. It turns out that "beer brand taste discrimination" was a rather large area of research. Looking back, I guess I should not have been surprised since there is so much money in the beer market.

In my favorite study, the researchers recruited test families (not too difficult an area of research to recruit volunteers) and for three straight weeks, delivered two cases of beer every evening—six bottles each of four different beers, identified only by the color of the cap on the bottle, which they changed every day so that the test family would have to decide what they liked anew every day. The participants would leave the two cases on the porch the next morning—both the empties and the ones they had not drunk. The assumption was that they would drink more of the beer they liked best. The research question was whether or not their palates could discern enough difference among the beers for them to develop reliable and consistent preferences.

The results? People could discriminate between "regular" and "premium" beers. In other words, they could tell the difference between a Heineken and a Milwaukee's Best, and they had a definite preference for premium beers over regular ones, which came as no surprise. But *within* regular beers or *within* premium beers, they could not tell the difference. I would bet the house that nobody could consistently discriminate among a Miller Lite, Bud Light, and Coors Light without having identifying information. Their brand loyalty has not really developed through taste; it has been sold to them through advertising. In other words, rather than a preference for their brand being formed in their mouths, it was figuratively shoved down their throats. Even the beer you order is a performance.

And do not even get me started on Axe body spray. One advertisement featured thousands of bikini-clad beautiful women running at full speed with heaving breasts, climbing over mountains and swimming in the ocean to reach their object of desire: an ordinary-looking man standing on the beach spraying Axe into the air. The main target audience for these products is early adolescent boys. Do you think that there are a lot of 13- and 14-year-old heterosexual boys who are insecure about their attractiveness to girls? Clearly, this approach is way over the top, and even the least intelligent 14-year-old knows intellectually that a million women are not going to come running if he uses Axe. Or so I thought. One of my students told me that her younger brother had purchased his first can of Axe and returned home from school that day feeling very disappointed that he got no more attention from girls than he did on any other day.

But the absurdity of the claim does not matter all that much, because image is remarkably powerful. As pornography critic Gail Dines (2013) points out, it is relatively easy for people to be critical of messages delivered in text, but being critical of those conveyed through images requires some insight, training, and practice. If we saw a sign that said, "Women are worthless; use them up and throw them away," most of us would find it ridiculous and offensive, yet this is precisely the message that most pornographic images communicate. Likewise, imagine a beer ad with text on a blank screen that says, "You are not much of a man—not sexually desirable, masculine, powerful, or interesting. If you drink Miller Lite, you will be all of those things." It seems unlikely that this approach would be very persuasive, but people will buy the image that sells exactly the same message.

Remember the Bowflex exercise equipment commercials? Slow motion pictures of an incredibly buff young man flexing his muscles with the voiceover: "These could be your arms. These could be your shoulders. This could be your chest." The much less obvious subtext that could be added on at the end (best if read in an Arnold Schwarzenegger-type voice): "… if only you weren't such a scrawny, girly little man." For most ordinary men, those could not be their shoulders, arms, or chest.

And some ads are downright misogynist. Levi's Dockers ran an ad campaign called "wear the pants" than included this copy: "Once upon a time, men wore the pants and wore them well … Men took charge because that's what they did. But somewhere along the line the world decided that it no longer needed men. It's time to answer the call to manhood." Even more extreme, Dr. Pepper marketed a diet soda called Dr. Pepper 10 with the slogan "It's not for women." I tried to imagine a company marketing a product with the slogan, "it's not for Jews." Or "it's not for Latinos." Again, most people know by now that they are not supposed to be racist, but sexism is still an acceptable social activity. Marketers will stop using it when people are offended and refuse to buy the product, but that, of course will depend on our becoming aware of the harm and division that sexism fosters.

By the way, I am not pessimistic about this transformation taking place. I think that, despite the fact that racism and religious intolerance are not over by any means, we have come a long way toward acceptance in the past few decades. I have been amazed at the breakneck speed in which acceptance of sexual minorities has progressed in the United States. Ten years ago, 60% of Americans were against same-sex marriage, now 60% are for it. That is a sea change for a widely held discrimination based on a pervasive prejudice. Perhaps sexism is the next frontier. And it is clear to even the most casual observer that we need to redouble our efforts to end racism and religious intolerance, as we have seen a remarkable and disappointing backsliding in mainstream United States culture within the past few years.

Marketers want everything to be for sale: your body image, self-worth, sexuality, confidence, power, and value as a man. They do not want you to get any of these through relationships, introspection, skill development, or anything else they cannot sell you. Gail Dines (2013) says, "a substantial part of the American market depends on women hating their bodies." (Think diet plans, exercise equipment, makeup, and cosmetic surgery.) Likewise, a substantial part of the market depends on men having anxiety about their masculinity. In the process, marketers reinforce the malevolent fictions that discourage men from expressing themselves in all their depth and complexity. So, the next time you watch a gendered advertisement, ask yourself what is being sold as a lifestyle or value, and how is the product made desirable? What parts of myself am I being told that I should hate and suppress? How am I being manipulated?

But once in a while, there is a breath of fresh air. Beginning in 2013, a Guinness beer advertisement, which featured a group of men playing a very lively game of wheelchair basketball, began to air. The game is aggressive, joyful, and friendly. At the end of the game, all but one of the men stands up out of their wheelchairs and walk to the gym exit, and it becomes clear to the viewer that all of these men played from wheelchairs so that their one paralyzed friend could be included. It was so delightful to me to see masculinity associated with dignity, caring, and empathy. Could these more dignified images in advertising start a trend? I am skeptical. It takes a lot more creativity to write the Guinness commercial than it does to trot out the same tired hypermasculine stereotypes.

We have to ask ourselves: how manly is it to let others tell me how I should be—to give up a part of myself? I am in favor of expanding masculine values like courage, leadership, independence, and loyalty to apply them in situations where men have historically been culturally constrained. Many men think of courage as running into a burning building, which is courageous (assuming that someone is actually *in* the building). But is it not also courageous to say, "No, I'm not going to the strip club," "Pornography harms a lot of people, so I don't participate in it," or simply, "I like you; I'm glad you're my friend," rather than expressing affection indirectly through insults such as those comedian Rob Becker offered: "Still driving that piece of shit?"

Many men think that loyalty translates into "Anything my buddy does is alright with me." But if your buddy drinks 12 beers and tries to get behind the wheel of a car, or tells rape jokes, or takes risks with his body, and you do not try to stop him, that, to me is remarkably disloyal, and so we have to help men distinguish loyalty from conformity. Independence and leadership are attributes that allow a man to break conformity and do the right thing. Much more on this topic in Chapter 7.

This is not a self-help book. My goal is to tell you what I believe to be true, not what you should do about it. But I am going to break from that for just a moment and make one small suggestion to the men who are reading this book. Look around at your male friends, coworkers, teammates, relatives, and neighbors, and try to get inside their heads a little. Try to imagine what their inner lives are like, what parts of themselves that maybe they are not showing to you because they think you are not interested. Pick one or two men whom you are especially interested in getting to know better. And then figure out how you might invite them to tell you what is beyond their social performances. The results might surprise you.

# 5

# GOOD OLD DAYS

## The fiction of the bygone romantic era

Every so often, I encounter someone who laments about how much things have changed with regard to gender, ending with something like, "Wouldn't it be great to go back to a time when life was simpler and families were traditional?" Generally, they are referring to an idealized version of 1950s United States mainstream culture, when the dominant model was the (male) single wage earner and the (female) full time homemaker.

Would it be great? If so, for whom? Certainly not for women with career ambitions. Certainly not for men who wished they did not have to shoulder the burden of being the only economic provider in the family. Certainly not for people of modest means who needed two incomes to make ends meet. And by the way, also not for people who were not heterosexual, cisgender, white, or who otherwise had identities outside of the mainstream models. It turns out that this 1950s model was "traditional" only in the narrowest historical sense, and so it is important for students of gender studies to gain a historical perspective on how a gendered division of labor came about and what factors influenced it. And then, if we can understand these factors, we can make some informed prediction about where gender arrangements are likely to be in the future.

In 1986, Gerda Lerner published *The Creation of Patriarchy*, a historical examination of the factors that led to men's dominance over women in public life beginning some 6,000 years ago. She argued that gendered social arrangements are a product of a gendered division of labor that met the needs of most societies at the time. As you will see, this gendered division of labor is increasingly becoming a gendered *non*-division of labor. I am not so naïve to believe that the inequality between the sexes will be resolved during my lifetime or even during the lifetimes of any of my readers. After all, it took us thousands of years to get here and the system is not easily dismantled. But if one accepts the argument contained within this chapter, the conclusion is that progress, measured in the expansion of roles for both men and women, is inevitable given the factors that allow for more flexibility in our working lives, which will also lead to more flexibility in our lives outside of work.

We start with a very brief description of the great epochs of human labor. Everyone started out as hunter/gatherers. In fact, at least 98% of human existence was spent in these foraging societies. Then people learned how to grow food, domesticate animals, and stay in one place rather than roaming around looking for food that came solely from nature with no human intervention. At that point, agricultural societies began to dominate the world's economies, although foraging societies continued to exist (and still do in some parts of the world). As agricultural methods, especially machinery, developed so successfully, not everyone had to be farmers, as a small number of people could produce enough food for everyone. As Matt Ridley (2017) pointed out, a modern combine harvester can process enough wheat in a single day to make one-half million loaves of bread, which in pre-mechanized farming would have required the labor of a thousand people. Today, this quantity of wheat can be harvested even without a human operator because of advances in robotics. In fact, we now have more people in prison in the United States than we do farmers, a testament both to the remarkable efficiency of agriculture and to the horrible and unnecessary rise of mass incarceration.

As agriculture waned as the dominant mode of labor, a lot of work shifted to factories during the industrial revolution, although, obviously, farming-based societies continue to exist. And later even industrial societies have been supplanted in some parts of the world with post-industrial, information-based and service-based societies.

Lerner argued that, contrary to what many people believe, hunter/gatherer societies were much more gender egalitarian than agricultural ones. Those stories of cavemen hitting women over the head and dragging them away by their hair are modern-day extrapolations of something for which there is no evidence. (My little joke: the egalitarianism of foraging societies means that if you call a guy a Neanderthal, it's really kind of a compliment.) Since the survival of the group depended on cooperative foraging and sharing of food, and since women produced as much as 60% of the food supply, there was no need for them to do radically different work than men. To oversimplify the economic bases of these societies, food equaled wealth, and wealth equaled power, and so women were very important in their communities, as the survival of the group depended critically on their labor. And although food equaled wealth, food could not be stored for long periods of time, and so wealth could not be accumulated. Life in foraging communities was largely a day-to-day existence.

The gendered division of labor began to make its appearance in the dawn of agricultural societies for several reasons. First, food could be stored, which meant that wealth could be accumulated. As a result, children became an economic asset because they could start working in the fields at a young age and produce more than they could consume. Therefore, women who were able to give birth to many children also became an economic asset, as the means of production were intimately connected to the means of reproduction. And before the invention of labor-saving devices to make farming more efficient, men's upper-body strength also became an important resource. The best contribution men could make was to grow food and the best contribution for women was to have and care for many children. Men's province became the outside world; women's, the home. Or as Alfred, Lord Tennyson (1847/1891) put it, "Man for the field and woman for the hearth," and over time, men began to dominate in public life.

Another important factor in the shift from foraging to farming was that, rather than being nomadic, entire communities could remain in the same location for generation after generation. Land was valuable, private ownership emerged, and property and other assets had to be passed on to heirs, usually sons. Land also had to be defended from intruders, and so there were wars, which meant that some members of the community had to be willing to risk their lives. Until very recently, these tasks always fell solely to men, for several reasons. First, men do not become pregnant or nurse, and so they can range far from the home without disruption of the production and survival of children. Second, before the advent of modern weapons, upper-body strength was a significant war-making resource. And third, in some sense, men were expendable. If a lot of men die in a sparsely populated society, there are still enough to father more children, but if many women die, the society's potential for growth is significantly diminished.

Some scholars trace the origins of hegemonic masculinity to warrior culture. To be willing to die means to displace vulnerable emotions and instincts such as self-protection, and to be willing to participate in violence. To continue Tennyson's verse:

> Man for the field and woman for the hearth:
> Man for the sword and for the needle she:
> Man with the head and woman with the heart,
> Man to command and woman to obey;
> All else confusion.

And so, over time, women are forced to adopt a subservient role. Men adopt a dominant role, but at significant risk. Women's labor becomes largely unremunerated. Demographer and sociologist Stephanie Coontz, in two important works, *The Way We Never Were* (2016) and *The Way We Really Are* (1997) dispels the myth that women's labor was unimportant except for her child raising functions. Many families could afford seeds but not fresh produce; fabric but not ready-made clothing, and other raw materials, which women could transform into useable goods. Thus, their labor contributed to the survival of the family but was not directly tied to wage earning. Coontz (2016) also notes that, even in the heyday of the single wage-earner/full time homemaker model of the 1950s, only about 60% of children in the United States grew up in these families.

The pattern of the synchronized foraging-agrarian and male-dominated shifts even took place during the twentieth century among the African !Kung tribe (also known as the Ju/'hoansi) on the western edge of the Kalahari Desert. The tribe's movement from a foraging to an agriculture-based economy was accompanied by restrictions in women's mobility, sex segregation in children's groups, higher levels of aggression, and an increased unwillingness in men to do what came to be considered "women's work" (Basow, 1992).

As agricultural methods advanced in many parts of the world, the focus of work shifted from the farm to the factory, and at first industrialization did not do much to change the gendered division of labor, as men's upper-body strength was a considerable occupational asset before the advent of modern machinery. Fathers were at least in the vicinity of their households if they were farmers, but industrialization removed them from their homes for long periods of time (Keen, 1991), and masculinity became increasingly divorced from the domestic world. Parenting roles became even more polarized, with mothers taking care of children's emotional lives and physical needs, and fathers providing money and often meting out punishment.

Now men who worked in harsh industrial environments also had difficulty fitting in at home, and the early twentieth century saw a surge of "men's societies" such as the Masons and Elks, along with a sharp rise in university fraternity membership. These "homosocial preserves" (Kimmel, 2006) were both cause and effect of an even sharper separation of the sexes than was the case in agrarian-dominated societies. Although still somewhat popular, membership in these societies has steadily decreased and some now even admit women.

Many modern economies are now post-industrial, and as a result, the gendered division of labor is slowly becoming a gendered *non*-division of labor, for several reasons. First, we now live in an overpopulated world and children are not the economic assets they were in agrarian societies. In fact, they are quite the opposite. Almost any parent will tell you that children pose a financial burden, and so most families cannot afford to have more than a few children.

Those with access to reproductive technologies can also achieve a measure of control over whether they will have children at all, and if they do, how many they will have and how they will time the births of each. My mother, who was born in 1930, experienced eight pregnancies between the ages of 20 and 35; few women in the modern world now live their young adult lives that way. Although my parents had access to birth control, they did not use it because they believed it to run counter to their Catholic beliefs. Returning to Lerner's (1986) theory of the origins of patriarchy, as male domination began to take hold, it was also manifest in the "leading metaphors" of cultures, including religious ones. Goddesses became Gods based on the "counterfactual metaphor of male procreativity" (p. 220), and given the agrarian emphasis on women's reproduction, making the limitation of births a sin would seem to go hand in hand with male domination. Moreover, religious justifications have long been used to rationalize men's violence against women across a wide variety of religious traditions (See Johnson, 2015).

In the United States in the past few decades, social and religious conservatives have redoubled their efforts to prevent women from gaining access to reproductive technologies, in some cases, criminalizing those efforts, even to the point of suggesting that women who abort a fetus should be put to death (McCambridge, 2019). Progress is nearly always accompanied by backlash, as we can see in these sexist movements. These retrogressive efforts are also classist, as women with access to wealth also have a much easier time getting what they need and want than poor women, for example traveling to areas where they can legally abort if they live in places where they cannot. And, when poor women have more children than they can manage, they become even poorer.

The post-industrial world of paid labor has experienced, and will continue to have, remarkable transformations. We now have so many labor-saving devices that men's average advantage in upper-body strength is no longer an economic asset, and thus there is little work that men can perform and women cannot. This increasing non-division of labor even extends to military service, as war has become significantly technologized. A talented woman fighter pilot can perform as well as a talented man, and women have entered military service in unprecedented numbers in much of the world. Dual income families are very much the norm, and in many parts of the world, same-sex marriage and adoption are now legal, lending a legitimacy to alternative definitions of family as well as to the economic advantages that accompanies state-sponsored marriage, including legal protections, tax considerations, and access to credit and health insurance.

Thus, it appears that we may be slowly coming full circle from the gender egalitarian world that characterized early hominids, as men and women increasingly find themselves working together both inside and outside the home. Modern adults, especially those with modest or more considerable economic resources, have more options than ever to craft both their home and paid work force lives according to their values, interests, talents, needs, and situations, and gender is slowly becoming less of an organizing principle in divisions of labor.

The key word in the last sentence is "slowly." I am not suggesting that gender equality is anything close to becoming a "done deal." However, if I am correct it is inevitable in the very long run. We would do well to think in terms of the simultaneous processes of continuity and change. Yes, the military, highest levels of law, politics, corporations, and clergy are still dominated by men (this is continuity); but women have made significant inroads in all these areas (this is change). It took thousands of years to construct and maintain the gendered division of labor that has resulted in so many limitations for women and men (in that order) and these problems are not going to end tomorrow or even in our short lifetimes. But we will continue to expand opportunities beyond the arrangements that held when women and men traveled largely separate paths.

Alice Eagly and her colleagues (2019) provide compelling evidence of the simultaneous processes of continuity and change in their meta-analysis (a method of combining the results of many research studies) of 70 years of public opinion polls measuring gender stereotypes in the United States population. Over that period, women were increasingly seen as more communal (affectionate, emotional, and relationship-oriented) but judgments of men's and women's competence (intelligence and creativity) became much more equal. At the same time, there was little change in the belief that men were more agentic (ambitious and courageous) than women. The researchers attribute the shift in beliefs about women's competence to their increased participation in the paid labor force and higher education (a change), and yet, half of men and women would have to exchange jobs for the workforce to be fully sex-integrated (a continuity). These scholars also note that although women have entered previously male-dominated professions in unprecedented numbers, they have tracked into female dominated subfields in, e.g., medicine, where they are a disproportionate number of pediatricians and gynecologists, or business management, where they are a larger number of public relations and human resource officers than men. But the stereotype that men are more agentic than women continues to drive the male dominance in leadership positions, and thus discrepancies in average salaries and access to promotions, across many fields.

As workplaces have become more sex-integrated, people have become more aware of the problem of sexual harassment. The #MeToo movement that got renewed momentum with the exposure of sexual assaults by high-profile men such as Harvey Weinstein and Bill Cosby, and the sexual harassment complaints against those such as Bill O'Reilly and Mario Batali led the way in highlighting this awareness. Some men have not responded well to this renewed awareness and one can see in their resistance the assumption that women routinely lie about being harassed to advance their careers or gain revenge on men who have rejected them. One lawyer stated, "I don't work with women. If they're attractive, I'm too tempted. And if they're not attractive, what's the point?" (Grossman, 2017). I have heard quite a few male college professors state that they will never meet with a female student with the door closed and many corporate men say that they always have a third person present when they are meeting with a female subordinate. And in 2017, US Vice President Mike Pence stated that he never dines alone with any woman except his wife, a practice widely referred to as "the Pence rule," and he also never attends functions in which alcohol is served unless accompanied by his wife.

It seems to me that there are several possibilities of rationales for the Pence rule. One is that you do not trust women, believing that many would file a false report. And this is not merely that you do not trust some individual woman, who may have given you reason not to trust her, but that you believe that women as a group are untrustworthy and manipulative. A second possibility is that, like the lawyer quoted in the previous paragraph, you do not trust yourself, as if your sexual urges are not within your control. As I often ask: how does that work physiologically? Does the prostate exert pressure on the spinal cord, cutting off oxygen to the brain? And a third possibility is that your wife does not trust you, for which you may or may not have given her reason.

When I did a sexual harassment presentation for a law firm, one of the lawyers said that he uses the Pence rule for another reason: to protect the woman. Because this was on his anonymous feedback form, I was unable to follow up with him, but if I were, I would have asked, "protection from what?" If he were to conduct himself as a respectful human being, it would seem that she would need no such protection. The problem with the Pence rule is that, in business settings, it results in lower-ranking women having less access to high-ranking men that lower-ranking men have, which is discriminatory (Grossman, 2017).

There is little doubt that the workplace is changing and will continue to change, and clearly, the greater degree of contact between women and men in the workplace makes it likely that consensual relationships will emerge. So, what is a man to do if he finds himself attracted to an unattached co-worker? Liz Plank (2019a, pp. 211–216) offers a set of excellent guidelines. Her items are in quotes and followed by my comments:

1. "Take stock of how much power you have." Be very careful if there is a difference between you and the person in whom you have an interest.
2. "When trying to date a woman at work, use the rule of one." If you ask her out and she says no, do not continue to pursue her. If you follow the romantic comedy script and believe that persistence pays off, you are treading in dangerous territory. My former student Alison Green had a great definition of sexual pressure: "If I say no and you ask again, that's pressure."
3. "Be aware that if the attraction is mutual it's not harassment." Harassment is *unwanted* sexual attention. If you are "flirting" and the other person is not, it is not flirting. Workplace romances are not forbidden by law, although they may be by company or organizational policy. An exception is the fraternization rule in the US military which bans consensual relationships between service members of unequal ranks. It is incumbent upon the person giving the other this kind of attention to make sure it is not unwanted. And if you are trying to decide, make sure that you go back to guideline #1 and consider the compromised freedom to resist when a person is in a subordinate position.

Very few people wake up in the morning and say to themselves, "I am going to go into work today and be obnoxious, intrusive, and illegal." Harassers do not see themselves that way. They think that they are being cute, witty, and charming. But at least in the United States, the law is clear that one's intent does not define sexual harassment. Rather the law is defined by one's impact. Sexual harassment is any unwanted sexual attention in the workplace or any behaviors that create a hostile environment for either sex.

One important note: I have heard many men ask, "What if I slip and make an inappropriate comment? Are the 'sexual harassment police' going to come and take me away?" The answer is no unless that comment is a *quid pro quo*, which is a sexual extortion ("Have sex with me or you're fired") or bribery ("Have sex with me and I'll give you a raise"). A single instance of quid pro quo is legally actionable, but hostile environment harassment is only actionable if the behavior is severe, persistent, and/or pervasive. That inappropriate comment fits the definition of harassment, as it is sexual, unwanted, and in the workplace, but it is not actionable, although if you "slip," you would do well to apologize for your indiscretion and redouble your efforts to avoid repeating it. And by the way, "in the workplace" does not just mean in the *physical* workplace; it extends to social interactions with coworkers outside of work and to interactions on social media.

4. "You don't have to avoid women: Just stop harassing them." The problem is not (as in the Pence rule) women's presence, it is in the harasser's behavior.
5. "When it comes to chivalry in the workplace, ask if you're not able to tell." One should not assume that another wants their help, for instance with moving heavy objects. As I discuss elsewhere, this behavior can feel patronizing because of the suggestion that the woman is incompetent.
6. "Don't do anything for a woman that you wouldn't do for a man." As I also discuss elsewhere, I am all for politeness, civility, helpfulness, and respect, but I also feel strongly that it should take place outside the realm of gender.

What do all these occupational transformations mean for young men? On the one hand, their work and domestic lives will not necessarily follow a one-size-fits-all template. Some will find this change disconcerting; after all the "bygone romantic era" did confer a kind of certainty in how people would take their places in the adult world. But on the other hand, the expansion of opportunities allows men to be who they are first and to think about how they will fulfill masculine expectations second. One thing is certain: those who believe that they can follow their fathers' and grandfathers' formulas to live their lives are going to find doing so increasingly difficult. And if they fail to learn about and become critical of masculine cultural expectations, they will run the increased risk of being left behind in the modern world.

# 6

# A MAN'S GOTTA DO WHAT A MAN'S GOTTA DO

## The fiction of violence

I begin by citing two indisputable facts:

1. The vast majority of men and boys are never violent, and
2. Men and boys commit a large majority of violent acts.

Over the years, I have spoken with many people who struggle to hold these two statements in their consciousness simultaneously. One common reaction to the second statement above is the accusation of "male bashing." "You're saying there is something wrong with men," "You hate men," and even "You hate yourself." I can assure you that I do not hate men, and unless I am being remarkably self-delusional, I also do not hate myself. In fact, I think we will have come a long way toward solving the problem of violence when we associate being a man with complexity, dignity, empathy, and respect. And I am also not saying that there is something wrong with men—read statement number one above. I am saying that there is something wrong with violent men.

Another resistant statement is, "Women are violent too." Without a doubt, this is a true statement, and we need to hold every violent person accountable for their actions. But the fact that women's violence is much less frequent than that of men tells us that violence is a gendered issue and that if we want to reduce the problem, we need to pay attention to its gendered aspects. And, when I say, "A lot of men are violent," and you respond with "But women are violent too," you are changing the subject. Here is a parallel:

Following the acquittal of George Zimmerman for the shooting death of Trayvon Martin in 2013, the international activist movement Black Lives Matter developed to protest systemic racism and violence against people of African heritage, especially in the United States by white police officers. This form of protest became even more pronounced following the 2020 killing of George Floyd by a white police officer. In response, the phrase "All lives matter" sprang up as a form of resistance. I began to think of the logic of such a response, and I think the following parallel is instructive.

To take it out of the realm of race and gender, suppose that you make a claim such as "Football is a great sport," and I respond with "Baseball is a great sport." I am not really responding to your assertion; I am changing the subject. You would do well to offer the rejoinder, "I did not say anything about baseball; I am talking about football." If you disagree with the statement about football, the only logical response would be to mount an argument that football is *not* a great sport. And there are arguments to be made there, especially considering what football does to a lot of men's brains and bodies. To say, "Baseball is a great sport" as an argument against the assertion that football is a great sport is a coded response that either means "Football is not," or "I like baseball better."

But, if instead of saying that football is a great sport, I had said that football is the *greatest* sport, then baseball and every other sport are on the table for discussion and argument. Likewise, if you respond to "Black lives matter" with "All lives matter," you are changing the subject. I did not say that other lives did *not* matter, I said that black lives *did*. The only logical counterargument to "Black lives matter" would be to assert that black lives *do not* matter, and that is a racist argument. And so, I believe that asserting "All lives matter" in response is code language for either "Black lives do not matter," or "white lives matter more than black ones."

Likewise, if I say that men's violence is a problem and you respond with "Some women are violent too," that tells me that you do not want to deal with the large difference in violent behavior between the sexes. As with many issues, resistance often takes the form of citing individual exceptions to systemic phenomena.

On the other hand, I also get some resistance from people who are all too familiar with the problem of men's violence. Focusing on the first statement, that most men are not violent, they say, "You are downplaying the problem of men's violence." I am trying very hard not to do so, which is why I make the second statement that most violent people are men. I try to be clear that violence is without a doubt a gendered problem. The suggestion that I am minimizing men's violence sometimes embodies the belief that it is natural and inevitable. Although men and boys commit a large majority of violent acts (Federal Bureau of Investigation, 2016), the vast majority of men are not violent. We also know that violent people are much more likely than others to have had adverse childhood experiences, to consume violent media, and to hold violence-justifying attitudes (Smiler & Kilmartin, 2019). These factors are changeable, and even if males are somewhat biologically predisposed to physical aggression (see the discussion of that issue in Chapter 3), reducing these experiential influences will go a long way toward minimizing violence.

You may be wondering at this point that since I have asserted that most violent acts are committed by males, why the chapter title mentions "the fiction" of violence. It is not a fiction to say that violence is primarily a gendered phenomenon. The fiction is the belief that men and boys are naturally violent. After I make the argument that violence is neither natural nor inevitable, I will turn to the problems of how we prevent and respond to men's violence, an endeavor in which I have been involved for more than 30 years.

Returning to the old nature/nurture debate, many argue that, since men-as-a-group are more violent than women-as-a-group, there must be something biological that predisposes men to physical aggression. The leap to biology is seductive because it is the most obvious possibility for many people. But human beings are, more than any other animals, creatures of experience. It could be that there is a biological predisposition to violence, but it also true that cultural influences have the power to restrain or to potentiate that predisposition.

The inevitability argument falls short on one piece of very strong evidence: the vast majority of men are never violent. If physical aggression is innate in men, then we must be doing something culturally to restrain this preponderance of men from this supposedly natural behavior. If, however, there is nothing natural about violence, then there must be cultural forces that impel a minority of men to wreak intentional harm on others. I find the second possibility more compelling. If we investigate the backgrounds of violent men, we find some combination of thoughts, feelings, and experiences that we do not see in normal and healthy men.

To be fair, the biological argument may have some merit. Males as a group have higher physical activity levels than females (with, as always, great individual variation) and there may be some connection there to aggression. Biological predispositions create thresholds for behavior. Experiences can create influences that either encourage or discourage the crossing of these thresholds.

To again take it outside the realm of violence, here is an example of two fictional characters with very different predispositions. The British spy James Bond has been a cinematic staple for decades. He can have a thousand people shooting at him but he remains calm at all times. Contrast James with the character George Costanza from the television show *Seinfeld*. Everyday life is upsetting enough for George. James Bond is extremely unlikely to develop an anxiety disorder. It could happen if, for instance, he was exposed to severe trauma. On the other hand, it does not take very much to frazzle George's nerves.

It could be that there is a small minority of men who, due to physiological abnormalities, are extremely prone to violence. For instance, there is some evidence that people (who are mostly males) with *antisocial personality disorder* have deficits in certain areas of the brain that are associated with impulse control, and this disorder has moderate heritability. If both parents had the disorder, the chances of their child having it is significantly increased even if the child is not raised by the biological parents. But antisocial personality disorder is relatively rare, and so we cannot explain the preponderance of male violence with these somewhat unusual cases. When we look at the big picture of male violence, this disorder adds little to our understanding. And even if we see brain abnormalities in some violent men, there is the possibility that rather than, or in addition to, the abnormalities being innate, the brain may be altered by experiences such as trauma. Too often we forget that experience changes the brain.

One compelling piece of evidence that physical aggression is not "hard-wired" into males is that sex differences in harming behaviors do not appear until preschool age. There is no hormonal event that can provide a basis for the explanation of how this sex difference begins to emerge at that time. Gender socialization and expectations are much more plausible as the major factor. By middle school, boys engage in physical fights twice as often as girls and are twice as likely to threaten others with physical harm (Smiler & Kilmartin, 2019). And they are also much more likely to engage in criminal behavior if they associate with peers who do so (Huizinga, Weiher, Espiritu, & Esbensen, 2003). Overall, men and boys commit nearly 90% of violent crimes (Federal Bureau of Investigation, 2016).

In the end, the argument is somewhat moot. Is it nature or nurture? The answer is nearly always "yes." Some people are highly predisposed to aggression and it takes little to push them over the threshold. Most, however, are not, and so the "push" must be much greater to cause them to be intentionally harmful. As I said in Chapter 3, I think it is ethically problematic to alter someone's biology to bring their behavior under control. But we can do something to reduce the cultural influences that impel violence, and in the remainder of this chapter, I will explore the gendered dimensions of these influences and offer some insights into how we might take steps to respond to and prevent the incidence of physical aggression.

Men who conform to the dominant social pressure to be stereotypically masculine are much more likely than other men to be violent (Cohn & Zeichner, 2006). Perhaps the worst insult one can give to a boy is to suggest that he throws, dresses, acts, or otherwise behaves like a girl. Thus, masculinity is defined as anti-femininity and boys learn from an early age to avoid any behaviors associated with girls and women. Physical aggression is one way of demonstrating anti-femininity through the domination of others, and the use of violence is culturally reinforced in sports such as boxing, football, and mixed martial arts, and in television and cinema portrayals of police, military, and "action heroes." Mainstream culture has a love/hate relationship with violence. On the one hand we decry it. On the other, we revel in the violence of some sports and gravitate to media portrayals of it.

One aspect of culturally defined femininity is the display of vulnerable emotions, and so men who conform to anti-feminine belief systems learn to convert these emotions into anger, which, along with lust, is seen as acceptable for men. So that if a conventionally masculine man feels threatened, sad, or worried, he often feels angry and reacts with aggression, which is sometimes physical. And in contrast to vulnerable emotions, which are considered to under complete control for men, anger is seen as being completely out of control.

One common form of violence is Intimate Partner Violence (IPV), also known as Domestic Violence (DV), in which a (usually male) offender brings intentional harm against a relationship partner. Most of these men are not violent outside the home, so what is the gendered connection? John Lynch and I (Lynch & Kilmartin, 2013) have written about what we termed "the masculine dilemma: not too close, not too far away." Within relationships, some men feel extreme conflicts between their feelings of dependence (which is culturally defined as feminine) and the masculine demands for dominance and independence. When his partner feels too close, he may behave aggressively to push them away, but then the dependency needs begin to arise as the partner now feels too far away, and so he brings them back in through the "honeymoon" phase. This cycle of violence continues and often escalates in the absence of psychological intervention. Donald Dutton (2011) calls men's interpersonal violence the product of "anger born of fear." And we should not forget that this domestic violence often takes place in a social context in which women are often blamed for their own victimizations at the hands of their male partners, and within cultural systems that devalue women's experience (Kilmartin & Allison, 2007).

What can we do about the problem of men's violence? I will use the remainder of this chapter to construct a model that guides us toward the understanding of this phenomenon and then another that guides us toward solutions. Nearly all my work in this area has been around gender-based violence—sexual assault, domestic (intimate partner) violence, and sexual harassment in the workplace, and so in most of what follows I concentrate on those forms of violence.

Sexual harassment and assault are caused by a variety of individual, subcultural, and cultural factors, and so we must intervene at all these levels to do effective prevention and response. As I have written elsewhere (Kilmartin, 2014), we can picture the problem as an interaction of individual factors with social and cultural ones. Picture a pyramid shape with low numbers of people at the tip and more people and larger social structures as you move from top to bottom. The base supports the rest of the structure.

At the tip of the pyramid are the offenders, a fairly small group of people, the vast majority of whom are men. With regard to sexual assault, most offenders victimize multiple women (Foubert, Clark-Taylor, & Wall, 2019), so relatively few men are rapists, but those who are show a strong tendency to assault again and again. At the next level down are what I term "direct facilitators," most of whom are men, who have relationships with the offenders. These men do not commit crimes, but they support the perpetrators by, for instance, showing their approval for disrespectful jokes or comments about women, harassing women in public, being passive when they see the offender grooming or overpowering a victim, or failing to cooperate if the offender is reported and investigated.

As anthropologist Peggy Sanday (1981; 1996; 2007) has noted, sexual assault is quite rare in many cultures, evidence that social forces are also in play in those which she terms "rape-prone" societies. The third level of the pyramid is comprised of people who have great influence over large audiences. The term I use to describe these people is *cultural standard bearers*, many of whom have a strong media presence. They may publicly downplay the horror of violence, suggest that someone reporting victimization (especially by someone famous) is lying, or make comments that are sexist, and/or those that espouse rape myths such as the belief that the person reporting was cooperative but later regretted consenting and reported that she had been assaulted to gain some financial or social advantage—the "buyer's remorse" argument.

For example, in March 1977, then 43-year-old film director and producer Roman Polanski arranged to be alone with a 13-year-old aspiring actress. He gave her alcohol and barbiturates and penetrated her orally, vaginally, and anally. Charged with five very serious offenses, he pleaded guilty to a lesser charge of indecent liberties with a minor child. Before he was sentenced, he fled to France, from where he could not be extradited to the United States. Thus, he became a fugitive from justice. He traveled to Switzerland in 2009, where he was detained, and the United States, which has an extradition treaty with the Swiss, requested that their law enforcement personnel be permitted to take him into custody.

A Swiss court ultimately rejected that request but the possibility that Polanski might return to face sentencing for the crime to which he pleaded guilty and for his illegal flight brought this case back into the public eye. Cultural standard bearer Whoopi Goldberg on the popular daytime television show *The View* stated that Polanski was not guilty of "rape-rape," (The Guardian, 2009) thus downplaying the significance of the sexual victimization of a young girl. A number of other media figures also defended Polanski.

More recently, when Donald Trump nominated Brett Kavanaugh to the Supreme Court of the United States in 2018, Dr. Christine Blasey Ford came forward at the Senate hearings to report that Kavanaugh had sexually assaulted her. Many lawmakers as well as other influential members of Trump's political party used their platforms as cultural standard bearers to either portray Ford as a liar and/ or to downplay the significance of sexual assault (The New Yorker, 2018). Incidences of cultural standard bearers supporting rape are so numerous that they could fill volumes.

The next tier of the pyramid is the widespread phenomenon of cultural sexism, the disrespect of women. In the aggregate, sexism is a system that is both reflected and reinforced by social practices and institutions that place women at risk of a variety of negative outcomes. For example, about 50% of women who serve on university faculties in United States STEM (science, technology, engineering, mathematics, and medicine) fields report having been subject to sexual harassment during the three-year period leading up to an extensive survey. Factors related to an elevated risk of being harassed include the perceptions within a work environment that complaints will not be taken seriously, that reporting harassment entails significant risk, and that harassers routinely escape accountability (Episode 16, 2020). When I spoke about men as allies to women in STEM at Princeton University in 2016, I also had the opportunity to meet with graduate students. One advanced physics student told me that she had recently made the very difficult decision to leave the field because she could no longer tolerate the hostile environment, thus the field lost a talented and well-trained person. To their credit, Princeton and other institutions have made strides toward addressing the problem, such as the implementation of codes of conduct, and hiring and promotion practices that safeguard the community (Episode 16, 2020).

At the base of the pyramid are the inequality and power differences between the sexes. In her landmark work, *The Creation of Patriarchy*, historian Gerda Lerner (1986) wrote that systemic male dominance over women has the effect of relegating women-as-a-group to a condition of "relative un-freedom" compared with men-as-a-group. You will note that I use the hyphens here to emphasize that there are great individual variations within each group. As Lerner points out, advantages to members of dominant groups have never accrued to every member of that group in equal measure, nor have disadvantages to every member of a subordinated group.

The problem of men's violence toward women is multifaceted and involves social and cultural practices. Therefore, solutions to these problems require that we deal with and dismantle every level of the pyramid.

## What do we know about offenders?

Beginning at the top of the model involves describing offenders. Once we know what impels them to violence, a public health approach entails reducing those factors within the population, which should result in a reduction of that violence in the aggregate. The first thing we know about offenders is that they have different experiences and characteristics compared with normal and healthy men. Cognitively, they often believe myths about rape, such as that a woman cannot be raped without her cooperation and that women routinely lie about being assaulted because of regret or embarrassment, or that they do so to seek vengeance upon men who have rejected them.

Before going on with the characteristics of offenders, I think it is important to address the myth that women routinely lie about being raped. A myth does not have to be untrue in all cases to be a myth; certainly, some women lie about being assaulted. But the power of a myth is in *how it functions*. Lying about an assault is quite rare, but the belief that it is commonplace allows the myth to function in a way that makes disbelief of the victim the default option, thus putting her in the position of having to prove her honesty. We do not do this with any other crime. Certainly, people have also lied about being robbed, but most people, upon hearing the report of a robbery, do not assume it is a lie and thus look for discrepancies in the victim's account that might expose the lie.

In an outstanding training for law enforcement personnel that is available online, psychologist Rebecca Campbell (2012) describes the effects of trauma on the brain, specifically the memory system. In the immediate aftermath of an assault, memories tend to be fragmented and come out in a non-linear fashion. When many untrained police detectives listen to a victim's account, they become skeptical of her honesty when the narrative changes and details are added later. They tend to think, "She can't get her story straight; she must be lying." Campbell explains how brain events following trauma lead to memory disruption, and thus a non-linear and fragmented memory is much more the rule than the exception. And, according to the research, memories recalled hours or days later are reliable unless the victim was drugged or unconscious at the time of the attack. Campbell's recommendation is that detectives re-interview the victim a few days later after she has had some time to recover the memories. We also know that the rapid eye movement (REM) cycle of sleep is essential to memory consolidation and so one or more periods of sleep will aid in recall.

The stereotype of sexual assault is one in which a rapist waits for a stranger to enter an isolated area and overpowers her, sometimes with the use of a weapon. But in most cases of sexual assault, the attacker is known to the victim. In many cases, victim and/or offender had been drinking prior to the attack, and in some cases, the victim was attracted to the offender. She may have consented to kissing him but he overpowered her when she refused to go further. If we believe that victims routinely lie, we should ask ourselves, if she is trying to convince someone that an event took place when in fact it never did, why did she not tell a story that is consistent with the stereotype? Why would she say, "I liked him; we were having drinks together; I kissed him, but didn't want to have sex," rather than, "He pulled out a gun, held it to my head, and threatened to shoot me if I didn't cooperate?" We should also ask, "When did I or someone I know ever falsely report that someone had committed a serious crime because I was embarrassed at my own behavior or wanted them to suffer?"

One more myth that we should also explore is the belief that if the victim did not physically resist, then she was complicit. But as Rebecca Campbell (2012) also points out, many victims show a tonic immobility, or "freeze" reaction, an involuntary brain response that renders them incapable of resistance. You may recall a time when something happened that so surprised and stunned you that you were unable to move or speak.

Here is my experience of a freeze response: one day I was at a supermarket, and when I got into my car to come home, I was backing out of a parking space and a car on the other side was doing the same. The driver obviously did not see me and was coming toward my car. They did not stop when I blew the horn. The solution to avoiding an accident was simple; I merely had to put my car into drive and return to the parking space that I was backing out of, but I completely froze, sitting there and thinking I was going to be hit. Fortunately, the other car stopped inches away from me. I then drove home but felt like I was in a fog for over an hour. The lesson is this: if the prospect of a one-mile-an-hour automobile accident is enough to make someone freeze, imagine how likely it would be if you were in a social situation with someone you trusted and might have even been having fun, when suddenly that person became violent?

My friend and colleague Lisa Speidel is a faculty member at the University of Virginia and invites me to guest lecture in her classes several times a year. I suggested that she have her students watch Rebecca Campbell's (2012) on-line training, and it turned out to be transformative for one of her students who is a rape survivor. She had taken self-defense classes but did not attempt to fight off the attacker, and thus she engaged in a great deal of self-blame, believing that she was complicit in the rape, as is commonplace for both survivors and others. Once she learned about the tonic immobility response, she realized that she was not complicit and that she was not at fault, which very much accelerated her healing and recovery.

Sexual assault offenders also subscribe to sexist attitudes and the most destructive of masculine norms. They tend to believe that women and men are enemies (*adversarial sexual beliefs*), that women being empowered leads to men being disempowered (*zero sum sexual beliefs*) (Wong, Klann, Bijelic, & Aguayo, 2017), and that they are entitled to sex. Perhaps the most disturbing product of this entitlement is the "involuntary celibate" ("incel") social movement. Its participants are unable to find women to love and have sex with them, and instead of exploring the reasons for their problem in their own behavior and attitudes, or dealing directly with their disappointment and sadness, they convert their vulnerability to anger and their entitlement into "aggrieved entitlement" (Levant & Pryor, 2020), which justifies their blaming women for their problems (vox.com, 2019). At the extreme are participants of the movement who have committed serious acts of violence, including mass murders of women.

As activist and former professional football player Joe Ehrmann (2011) often says, "Hurt people hurt people." It is clear that nearly all people who commit violent acts have suffered their own trauma, often in childhood. I hasten to add again that having been victimized in no way justifies or excuses their behavior unless they are so psychotic that they cannot distinguish right from wrong. But if hurt people hurt people, we can prevent the harm that they do by safeguarding them, or if they are victimized, by helping them recover from trauma in healthy ways.

If someone is keenly aware of the pain that results from being mistreated, we would think that they would be the last person to commit a violent act, and that is true for most survivors. David Lisak (1997) described the process by which a man who was hurt as a boy becomes an abuser as an adult. They have failed to address and cope directly with their childhood trauma. Doing so requires them to experience vulnerable emotions such as sadness, anxiety, and worry, but if they subscribe to the masculine tendency to associate these feelings with weakness and femininity, they cannot experience these feelings directly nor ask for help.

According to Lisak, there seems to be two paths for the traumatized boy. He can acknowledge his victimization and deal with it directly by rejecting the masculine demands for control and the eschewal of the feminine. This process may leave him with what we might term "conventional" symptoms: depression, anxiety, post traumatic reactions, etc. The other path is to accept these masculine demands and convert his feelings into anger, the masculine "emotional funnel system" (Long, 1987). Aggression is the most common behavioral by-product of anger.

The second and sometimes overlooked factor in offenders is the decision to act violently. Even if one has a history of childhood adversity, they are still bear the responsibility for what behaviors they choose unless, as I have already stated, they are so mentally impaired that they cannot distinguish right from wrong. There is no contradiction between understanding someone's pain on the one hand and holding them accountable for their behavior on the other.

The means to do harm is the third factor. In acquaintance assault situations, most offenders use upper-body strength, intimidation, misuse of authority, and other means to subdue victims. Sometimes victims are also impaired either by a drug like Rohypnol surreptitiously introduced by the offender, and/or with alcohol, which reduces their capacity to resist.

The fourth factor is the support of the offender's peers, and in fact, by the culture at large. When we look at well-known cases of perpetrators who have high levels of power and status such as film producer Harvey Weinstein, comedian Bill Cosby, or USA Gymnastics physician Larry Nasser, we see evidence that they their associates' actions or inactions allow them to operate with impunity for years. In more commonplace assaults, friends and attitudes factor into the violence. Offenders usually associate with those who pressure them into having impersonal sex with as many women as possible, who are uncomfortable when friends' make respectful and non-objectifying statements about women, who use sexualized language to describe women, and who believe that their friends endorse rape myths (whether they do or not) (Jacques-Tiura et al., 2015).

## Toward solutions

Many sexual offenders are repeat victimizers (Foubert, Clark-Taylor, & Wall, 2019). Can they be reformed? Unfortunately, we do not have any research of which I am aware that they can. In fact, I am not aware of any scholar offering approaches to treating them, although there is a literature for addressing perpetrators of intimate partner violence (see, e.g., Acker, 2013). Not everyone is a viable candidate for psychotherapy, including those with antisocial (sociopathic) characteristics, which are found in many serial offenders. The remaining recourses are unilateral ones: hold them accountable by, for example, terminating their employment or incarcerating them. But we know that friends matter and leadership matters, and when their peers and/or those who have power and status "rein them in" through bystander intervention and competent leadership, insisting that everyone in an organization participates and maintains respectful attitudes toward others, and when we hold offenders accountable, we can reduce the risk. With this strategy and the right training, we amplify the healthy voices of the majority of men who want to do the right thing, by transforming them from passive bystanders into active helpers. In training, we refer to allies willing to do this work as "upstanders" (as some people think that the term bystander implies passivity). Because men tend to have a lot of influence over other men, my research and consultation efforts have concentrated in addressing men to stand up for what is right.

A first step is to convince men that if they respect women and do not want to see anyone get hurt, they are not alone. Recall from Chapter 4 the study I did along with teams of student researchers, in which we demonstrated experimentally that interventions can help men to change their perceptions of others as well as of themselves by correcting men's overestimations of other men's sexism (Kilmartin et al., 2008), which may make it more likely that they will challenge disrespectful behaviors. As I also said in Chapter 4, men who behave in these ways do so because they believe that it will enhance their status with their male peers. It will stop when these comments instead meet with disapproval and loss of status with other men. And if we can change the perception that there are no allies in the room, other men will be more willing to follow suit.

A second study (Kilmartin et al., 2015) was inspired by the research on factors involved in changing people's attitudes. It is quite obvious that people think about their attitudes while making decisions about how to act, but we also know that people self-observe their behavior in discerning what their attitudes are (Aronson, 2001). We can actually change someone's sense of what they believe by getting them to act in a way that is consistent with the attitude, even as an exercise. I call this an "outside-in" change. For example, if you are able to get someone to display a yard sign supporting some cause, it is more likely that they will take action in the direction of the cause that the sign supports (Aronson, 2008), as public commitment increases private acceptance. The exception is that change is less likely if the person is given a large reward for displaying the attitude. If you give the person $1,000 to display the sign, they are less likely to change than if you give them a small amount or no money at all. The large reward effect is that people can then attribute the display to the reward rather to their own values.

Our second project was an attempt to effect an "outside-in" change in sexist attitudes. It was inspired by a very successful intervention in another domain: eating disorders. Eric Stice and his colleagues (2008) identified high school girls who were at risk of eating disorders and then randomly assigned them to two groups. In the intervention group, the girls designed posters criticizing unhealthy eating patterns and the cultural standards of thinness for girls and women. They also role-played scenarios in which they challenged a friend who was eating unhealthily. The team found that just a few hours of this work made it much less likely that they would develop eating disorders years later, compared with the control group who received no treatment.

We wanted to see if having men practice a scenario in which they challenged a peer's sexist behavior would actually have the effect of increasing their own respect for women. And so, we assembled small groups of male college students who participated in exchange for course credit. As in the first study, we measured sexism, rape supportive attitudes, and level of comfort with other men's sexism. We randomly assigned them to the experimental or the control groups.

In the experimental groups, we directed them to imagine that they were in a group of men when one member of that group makes a sexist comment or joke; we displayed specific examples on a screen and had them take turns in the role-playing exercise. After we put each sexist comment on the screen, we told them that it was offensive to them and then they took turns coming up with challenges to the hypothetical man who made the comment. (We did not ask them to respond *if* they were offended; we wanted to subtly suggest that a respectful reaction is normative, which it is even if they think otherwise.) And because they did this exercise in groups, they also got to experience other men as models for confrontation of sexism.

In the control group, the scenarios were constructed around a peer who was not being assertive, and we asked the participants to role-play a challenge to his failure to stand up for himself. We told them that we would re-assemble the group later, and we asked them to write a hypothetical letter to the unassertive or sexist man in the interim and bring it with them at follow-up. We gave them this assignment because we wanted them to spend at least a little time thinking about the issues in the interval between meetings.

Three weeks later, they returned and we gave them the same surveys they had completed in the first sessions. Those who had practiced challenging sexism had a small but significant reduction in their own levels of sexism. As we expected, there was no change in sexism for the men who had challenged a peer's lack of assertiveness. Therefore, the effect in the experimental group was due to our intervention and not just because they changed merely in reaction to having completed the surveys. This was a very brief intervention (less than 30 minutes) and so we were pleased that doing something so modest could produce a measurable effect.

The great social psychologist Elliot Aronson (2001) stated that the overarching lesson of his career was that people were more likely to change, and that if they did, the change would last longer, if they believe that they had persuaded themselves rather than being "talked into" the change by someone else. Both this experiment and the social norms intervention that I described in Chapter 4 were efforts to take men through a process that would result in an attitude change rather than having someone tell them what they should think or do.

I think it would be quite naïve to suggest that these two techniques could change men forever. However, I hope that researchers with access to greater resources (such as graduate students and funding) will extend this work. In the big picture, true cultural change involves much bigger social systems than a few men who spend a little time in a psychologist's laboratory. But cultural change in possible, and within organizations, leadership matters a great deal. For instance, the most important finding around military sexual assault is that when a commander communicates that they are comfortable with a hostile work environment for women, or worse, when they actually participate in establishing and maintaining that climate, women who work for them are six times more likely to suffer sexual assault than women who work for commanders who set a tone of respect for women (Sadler et al., 2003). The parallel for the sexual assault of men is the connection between a commander's endorsement of hazing and men's elevated risk, as most military men who experience sexual assault are being hazed at the time (Farrell, 2015). Likewise, organizational tolerance of disrespect, which is strongly influenced by leadership, is the single most important factor associated with high rates of sexual harassment (Willness, Steel, & Lee, 2007).

These data are correlational, and one mantra of general psychology is that "correlation does not imply causation." There could be some other factor that systematically co-varies with hostile work environment or hazing that causes the elevated risk, but it is hard for me to imagine what it might be. I certainly think that the relationships are causal. If so, we can dramatically reduce soldiers' risk of sexual victimization if we can remove commanders who have these dangerous attitudes, and if we employ effective leaders who set the example and the expectation of a respectful workplace culture. In fact, those processes are well underway. In the United States, sexual victimization of military personnel dropped by more than half within a single decade (2006–2016) (Sapr.mil, 2020).

The military collects data on victimization experiences every two years. Many of us who work in this area were profoundly disappointed when there was an increase in cases from 2016 to 2018. What could be the factors that fueled this backsliding? I can only speculate, but that increased risk also came at a time when there was a very noticeable increase in the mainstream acceptance of disrespect, including the rise of overt racism and sexism. A major cultural standard bearer of this change was the president who took office in 2017. More than 20 women have reported that he assaulted them, and he is also first in command of the Armed Forces.

## The big picture of solutions

Violence is obviously a profound ethical issue and we need to teach people about the moral dimensions of intentional harm of another human being. However, my experience as an educator is that the moral discussion is a poor entry into the topic. When people first began to talk to men about rape, some educators began their discussions with men by suggesting that all are potential rapists and warning them that they would be punished severely if they did not behave correctly. Understandably, men were offended at the approach and tended to move in the direction of less rather than more empathy for victims.

A much better entry into the topic is enlightened self-interest approach. Rather than suggesting that people are by assumption bad actors, we try to get them invested in the issue by helping them understand that they have something to gain by learning about it. Once they understand that a change will bring benefit to them, and that we, as educators, are trying to help them and enlist them as allies, they are more prepared to deal with the moral issues. To be clear, I am not saying that educators should not discuss the morality of violence—they absolutely should—just that leading with it has great potential to backfire by engendering resistance. In the enlightened self-interest approach, we display empathy for our audiences by asking about their goals and values. Then we help them to understand that the prevention of maltreatment is entirely in concert with these goals and values.

An illustration: on my campus there were well-substantiated rumors that a faculty member had engaged in serious sexual misconduct with a student. During the time when the student's complaint was being investigated, the faculty member decided to resign, as he had secured another job. Once he did, the investigation was over from the college's point of view, although the student would have been able to pursue a criminal or civil complaint if the offense was more than a violation of organizational policy.

A few years later, I was astounded to see this now-former professor in the faculty lunchroom, and so I asked one of his department colleagues why he was there. The colleague told me that they had a position open, that the former department member had applied, that he was a finalist for the job, and that he was on campus for an interview. I wanted to express outrage but did not, calmly asking the colleague what the chances were that they would re-hire him. The colleague basically said that there was little doubt that they would. I decided that I needed to communicate with the Dean of the Faculty.

Had I taken the morality approach, I would have expressed outrage that they would even consider this person given the gravity of the complaint. Of course, the Dean was not someone who was comfortable with people being hurt, but that problem was not foremost on his mind; his job was to run the academic side of the college. I instead took the enlightened self-interest approach by asking myself what the Dean's goals were. One of them is to avoid legal entanglements whenever possible.

Because I had led all of the sexual harassment prevention training on campus, I was well aware of the law and of the college's responsibilities, and so in my email to the Dean I said,

> I noticed that former Professor "X" was on campus today and one of his colleagues informed me that he is a finalist for a position. I have it on good information that, before he resigned, there was a very serious sexual misconduct complaint against him, and so I am concerned about our legal exposure here. When an organization knew or should have known about harassment and does not take all reasonable steps to remedy it and prevent its recurrence, that "deliberate indifference" can be the basis for a lawsuit. And so, absent a resolution of the complaint, and evidence of his rehabilitation if the complaint is sustained, we put ourselves at great risk.

I was informed a few days later that the candidate had "withdrawn" his application.

When I train people who work for businesses, after helping them understand the law and the behaviors that constitute sexual harassment, I ask, "How can sexual harassment harm your business?" Usually, the first thing that comes up is the potential for being sued. I respond by describing some lawsuits that some corporations have settled for tens of millions of dollars and get them to think about how much productivity and sales it would take to make up such a large amount of money. This approach appeals to their enlightened self-interest, as the main goal of most businesses is financial profit.

The loss of a lawsuit creates obvious and direct costs, even occasionally resulting in layoffs and bankruptcies. But lawsuits are the tip of the iceberg, as they are relatively rare. There are also a great many indirect costs of which they should be aware. And so, I ask, "Have you ever had a job that you hated?" Most of us have. If you have not, you are very fortunate indeed. And so I then move to a discussion of how this dysphoric employment situation affected them. The most common answers:

"I got depressed (or even physically ill) and had to go for treatment,"
"Occasionally I called in sick when I wasn't,"
"I did the bare minimum; a good day at work was a day when nothing happened,"
"I did not care about the company; after all, they didn't seem to care about me,"
"I left work on the exact minute that my shift was over, even if I was doing something that I could complete in another few minutes," and
"I spent a lot of time looking for another job and quit as soon as I found one."

Nobody wants to spend a huge part of their lives in such discomfort, and we know from the research that sexual harassment poisons the work environment, resulting in lowered morale and productivity, greater absenteeism, higher health insurance costs, and more employee turnover, all of which compromise the business' "bottom line." But because, in contrast to the direct cost of a lawsuit, the everyday damage that harassment causes is indirect, it is often unnoticed. But when we add up these costs across all businesses, lawsuit expenses pale in comparison (Lawrence, 2020; Raver & Gelfand, 2005).

An employee does not have to be a direct target of harassment to be affected. Have you ever seen someone being mistreated and it bothered you, even though the bad behavior was not directed toward you? Those who witness harassment also suffer negative consequences. The effect is akin to second-hand smoke. Being in an atmosphere where toxins are present create problems even for those distal to the source of the poison. Therefore, it is in every employee's self-interest to participate in a fully respectful environment. And it is incumbent upon leaders to establish and maintain this positive workplace climate.

Several years ago, I teamed with Gail Stern and John Foubert to create the SHAPE (Sexual Harassment and Assault Prevention Education) program for the United States Naval Academy. We wrote sixteen one-hour lessons and trained peer educators to deliver them. Each lesson includes a discussion about the relevance of the content to their future positions as naval officers. For businesses, the enlightened self-interest approach is around profits; for military the appeal is to have maximum capacity to accomplish assigned missions. That goal is severely compromised when members are suffering trauma at the hands of their fellow troops. Harassment and assault severely compromise unit cohesion and can also result in skilled personnel resigning rather than re-enlisting after a tour of duty, a situation the military refers to as "talent bleed."

Once we have convinced people that they have the best chance of success when they pay close attention to these issues, we can move on to a discussion of the moral dimensions. If we can build empathy for everyone who has been directly or indirectly affected by mistreatment, we can help them become even more motivated to participate as effective allies in the efforts to build and maintain a fully respectful environment.

I firmly believe that trying to get people to have empathy for others begins with communicating that you have empathy for them. Indirectly, when we use the enlightened self-interest approach, we are saying that we understand what they value and want to help them to be successful. As I stated earlier, psychologist Rebecca Campbell (2012) trains detectives and police officers in understanding how sexual trauma affects the brain. This information helps them to be more thoughtful and thorough in their investigations, as they are encouraged to modify their interviewing approaches because they better understand memory disruptions and emotional effects. Their goal is to apprehend and convict criminals and so she is helping them become more sophisticated in doing so, but empathy for the victim is an unspoken by-product of the training. Understanding what is taking place in the brain of a sexual trauma victim entails imagining what they are going through.

As I also stated earlier, it is useful to think about sexual assault and harassment on multiple levels, which is why I use the pyramid model. This approach is also useful for thinking about solutions at multiple levels. As with the problem formulation on the pyramid, we can think of solutions in the same shape, with more people and bigger social forces involved from top to bottom. At the top of the pyramid are people who have a good deal of influence, such as business leaders, media figures, top military officers, and lawmakers, all of whom can use their considerable power and high levels of influence to affect the organizations they lead and even the culture at large.

Both the positive and negative possibilities for leadership were on display to me a few years ago when I visited three military bases in San Antonio, Texas, to deliver training for Sexual Assault Awareness and Prevention Month. My first presentation was at Fort Sam Houston Army Base. Personnel there organized and financed my visit and then "loaned" my services at no cost to the other two bases. In retrospect I realized that their organization was more invested in the events than those of the other bases, both literally in financial terms and figuratively in communicating the value of the activities. Base commanders generally have a discretionary personal budget, and the three-star general (the second highest rank in all the military) and top officer of the Fort Sam Houston Base used his personal budget to finance the events. He introduced me at the beginning of the training and paid close attention to what I had to say. Following the presentation, he restated some of the main points I had used and affirmed his commitment as a leader to making the base as safe and respectful as possible for all. He then posed for a photograph with me and gave me his personal coin (high ranking military have large coins struck to give to honorees). Everything he did conveyed the message that he took sexual assault prevention and response very seriously and that he fully expected that every soldier do the same. A visitor like me has limited capacity to influence (unless the visitor is famous, which I am not); it is up to local leaders with greater levels of influence to reinforce the visitor's presence and message. This leader did it as well as possible.

The next morning, I traveled to nearby Randolph Air Force Base to deliver a training to about 300 participants who were under orders to attend. Imagine my surprise when, at the appointed hour, the auditorium contained only about 75 people. It was obvious that, on that base, people knew that they could simply fail to show up for a training even though it was mandatory, and that if they did not attend there would be no repercussions. This laxity of discipline starts at the top and filters down through the chain of command to the rest of the personnel on the base, and thus the disobedience of the order to report to a mandated event, as well as the lack of accountability for those who missed it, were reflections of critical leadership failure. Things became even worse that same afternoon at nearby Lackland Air Force Base. Although the training was well publicized across the base, attendance was completely voluntary. The audience was comprised of only seven people.

As I reflected on my experiences at these three installations, I was struck by the remarkably stark contrast in how the leaders communicated the levels of importance they placed on the military-wide events of Sexual Assault Awareness and Prevention Month. At my first presentation, the organization, through its leaders, clearly communicated that these were important issues. At the other two bases, they merely scheduled events but did not invest energy and resources to leverage them to good effect. Lackland was the worst, of course, with the issue considered largely irrelevant from the top down through the chain of command. This poor leadership was exposed a couple of years later when there was a major sexual assault scandal on that base which resulted in removal of top officers and long prison sentences for the worst offenders.

When someone enlists in the Air Force, they first go to Lackland for seven and a half weeks to complete their basic military training. These recruits have the lowest levels of power of anyone in the service. They obey orders and have very little control of their lives. At Lackland, a significant number of military training instructors were using their power to sexually abuse recruits. The attacks were widespread, and so many instructors who were not assaulting recruits might well have known that others were. Because they failed to report their colleagues' criminal activities, their silence directly facilitated the activities of the offenders. Rather than helping to identify perpetrators and take steps to remedy current situations and prevent future ones, they allowed the problem to fester while so many more people were hurt, and until it exploded into a national scandal.

It was clear that there was a huge organizational problem at Lackland, and to learn from the scandal and prevent further damage to people and military units, a thorough investigation should involve going up the chain of command to find out how the leaders failed to manage the problem and to hold these top officers accountable for communicating dangerous attitudes and making poor decisions.

But generally, the problem is often treated like an individual rather than an organizational one and only identified offenders are held accountable. This approach results in a failure to address the larger issues of the cultural climate.

As we move down the pyramid model of solutions, we come to effective policies and well-trained responders. Most offenders attack more than one person, and so if we do not respond effectively to one attack, chances are that there will be others. Victim reports are critical because otherwise offenders are not identified. When there is a report, the failure of organizational and legal systems to respond effectively makes it more likely that there will be future victims. Effective response makes it more likely that future victims will report assaults.

There are facilitators and barriers to reporting an attack, and if we want to increase the rate of reports, we will have to enhance the facilitators and break down the barriers. It is a difficult task for a victim to come forward. Facilitators for their doing so include a sense that they will be safe, that they will be supported through the ensuing process, and that that process has a good chance to result in a favorable outcome. Some victims/survivors are also motivated by the belief that, if the offender is held accountable, they are much less likely to harm others. Barriers to reporting include not having the information they need, believing that the report will not be taken seriously, knowing that others who reported did not get justice and/or were mistreated and re-traumatized during the process, and not having the necessary services available to them.

As I stated, the United States military conducts surveys of all members every two years to discern the levels of sexual victimization and hostile work environment. Unlike their civilian counterparts, the military can require all personnel to participate, and so they have the clearest picture of the true incidence of these problems relative to reports. Technically, service members may sit at a computer during the assigned time but not complete the survey, but they are prohibited from doing anything else for that time period, and so the proportion of completion is nearly 100%. In non-military settings, researchers must ask people to participate voluntarily. At colleges and universities, which have an enormous problem with victimization, some have suggested that students be required to complete the surveys as a condition of being allowed to register for classes. This seems coercive, ironically, since we are asking about other coercive experiences, and so in many higher education settings, investigators try to offer positive incentives for participation. For instance, on my campus we offered doughnuts, among other things, to students who participated in the research.

Even with significant incentives, private sector climate survey compliance falls far short of military levels. In the most recent survey on my campus, participation was around 30%, and the investigators were pleased that it even reached that level. Fortunately, there are large-scale and well executed national surveys because of the pioneering work of psychologist Mary Koss and her colleagues (1987) although it is much more difficult to assess local levels of victimization. In some states, colleges and universities are now required by law to execute climate surveys and thus get an estimate of the levels of victimization and reporting on their campuses.

Because the military data are so complete, they have the best picture of the proportion of true incidents to reports, and that percentage tripled between 2012 (11%) and 2016 (32%). As I mentioned, 2018 data revealed a very disappointing increase in incidence, but at the same time the proportion of official reports to surveyed level of incidents held fairly steady at roughly one out of three (30%; Sapr.mil, 2020). Reporting levels at colleges and universities are much lower, with even large schools with tens of thousands of students receiving reports in the single digits, clearly far short of the true levels of incidence.

We can take a lesson from the military on how they were able to achieve a tripled reporting level in such a short period of time. Experts believe that the Victim Advocacy Program is the single largest factor. Rather than requiring a traumatized person to obtain their own medical, legal, and psychological services, the military now assigns a victim advocate, a well-trained expert who can help them get the support they need. For instance, in criminal hearings in the United States (including military courts), the system is designed to first and foremost protect the rights of the defendant. The victim is a witness to the crime. But an advocate can represent the victim in court and attempt to safeguard their rights as well as offer support during this very difficult process.

As we move down our pyramid model of solutions, the next level is environmental interventions. Because offenders attack much more often in some settings than in others, we can take steps to reduce their access to potential victims. This strategy has worked well with the problem of school bullying. Because incidents often take place in identifiable parts of the campus, such as locker rooms and isolated hallways, increased surveillance of these areas can result in lowered risk.

Recall the widespread problem of the sexual abuse of recruits at Lackland Air Force Base. Nearly all the offenses took place in the offices of the military training instructors, literally behind closed doors. These doors are no longer completely opaque, as windows have now been installed in them, thus making it highly unlikely that an instructor could meet with a recruit without being observed by supervisors or passersby (Instructors were also ordered to refrain from doing anything to obscure the view through the windows).

I often refer to Naval Station Great Lakes (near Chicago, IL) as the "poster child" of sexual assault prevention and response, as it achieved a 60% reduction of sexual violence over just a two year period by instituting a combination of leadership training, bystander intervention instruction, and an environmental intervention. Great Lakes is the Navy's counterpart to the Air Force's Lackland—the basic training site for all recruits. Like many military bases, the surrounding areas contain quite a few bars, and these environments can be hazardous. Thus, Great Lakes began patrols of local bars by under-cover military police trained to look for and intervene in dangerous situations.

As we continue toward the base of the pyramid, the next level involves training for all personnel: learning how to be an effective "upstander" who intervenes in potentially dangerous situations, participating by helping to establish and maintain a culture of respect and inclusion, and learning how gender expectations can contribute to violence. One major factor in men's sexual assault of women is sexism, which is a psychological prejudice. Thus, we can look to the research on prejudice reduction to form strategies.

The "contact hypothesis" is the belief that prejudice is reduced when people from different backgrounds, identities, and appearances have interactions with one another. It was the basis of a famous (and failed) social experiment in the 1960s United States after the Supreme Court ruled that public schools could not be segregated by race. Students from majority white schools were bussed to majority non-white schools and vice versa. And, in the words of Elliott Aronson (2001), who was in Austin, Texas at the time, "all hell broke loose." Students often self-segregated to, e.g., different sides of the school cafeteria, and there was a great deal of racial tension and violence.

It turns out that contact is a necessary, but not a sufficient condition for prejudice reduction. The most shameful chapter in United States history is the widespread capture and forced enslavement of African peoples. Under slavery, wealthy white plantation owners and their black slaves had a good deal of contact, but many, if not most white people maintained their dehumanizing attitudes toward enslaved and free blacks, and in some cases murdered them for any suggestion that they were challenging white authority. There was a good deal of contact but no prejudice reduction.

So, if contact is not enough, what else is needed? As Aronson (2001) demonstrated in an intervention with newly-integrated elementary schools in 1960s Texas, that contact needs to be among people of equal status and power who work together toward common goals in pleasant environments, and where they are dependent upon one another for both their individual successes and the success of the group. He demonstrated this effect using the "jigsaw classroom" technique where school children in integrated groups each learned one aspect of each lesson and then taught it to the others, whose grade depended upon learning a part of the curriculum from someone who did not look like them.

What does this research mean for the reduction of sexism and its most toxic byproduct, gender-based violence? If we can construct working groups in which there are significant numbers of both sexes, and those in which both sexes are well represented in positions of authority, and in which group members are interdependent, we should be able to reduce this prejudice. In many work environments, these conditions are slowly developing. As I noted in my discussion of the history and future of work in Chapter 5, the erosion of men's upper-body strength as an economic asset due to the rapid development of labor-saving devices, along with the fact that children are no longer an economic asset and coupled with the availability of reproductive technologies, means that there is very little work that men can do and women cannot. And most families need two incomes to sustain their lifestyles, thus we find men in traditional husband-wife families slowly taking on some of the domestic labor that was long the province of women. And in fact, the very definition of the family is changing beyond just two parents in a heterosexual relationship.

Back to the military—there are now more women members than ever. If we can reach a critical mass of them both organization-wide and within specific work groups and specialties, and if women become well-represented in leadership positions, we should see a continued reduction in sexism and gender-based violence.

Within the past 10–15 years, the United States military has been training every one of its members in learning how to be "upstanders"—noticing and intervening when dangerous situations arise. The fictional but widely accepted beliefs about men and women that I have described throughout this book can contribute to sexual assault and harassment, and so gender education is a key component to all violence reduction efforts, including bystander intervention.

The biggest challenge for solutions, and therefore the base of the pyramid, is to fundamentally change the culture to make respect, opportunity, diversity, and equally distributed power present both in individual attitudes and structural conditions and practices. As I mentioned in Chapter 5, the processes of continuity and change are simultaneous. Those who are invested in this biggest part of the picture must understand both processes. In the United States and many other parts of the world, for example, we now have greater representation of women as well as sexual, racial, and ethnic minorities in all sectors of public life such as business, politics, and law, an indicator that change is taking place. At the same time, that change is slow. Members of these subordinated groups are not even remotely represented in numbers relative to their actual proportions within the total population, an indicator of continuity. Being able to deal with both continuity and change is critical to working toward equality and to decreasing its most toxic by-products, violence and other maltreatment. If we only attend to the process of change, we may begin to believe that prejudice and inequality are no longer significant social problems. On the other hand, if we only notice continuity, we may come to believe that change is not possible. And so, the combined comprehension of change and continuity is critical for activists because it allows us to understand that the current system is both unfair, leading to a host of negative outcomes for members of some groups compared with others, and unstable, a system that can and does change.

## The effects of violent media

Violent narratives are fully imbedded in mainstream culture. For instance, although 0.2% of crimes committed in the United States are murders, fully 50% of those portrayed on television are. If violence were as common in real life as it is on television, it would take only 50 days to wipe out the entire population of the country (Bartholomew, Dill, Anderson, & Lindsay, 2003).

Although many people believe that these ubiquitous stories are harmless, more than 60 years of research demonstrates quite the opposite. Why do people believe that violent media has no effect? Perhaps because we have all experienced it, and most of us are not violent. But the evidence indicates that violent media increases the willingness to engage in physical aggression for those who have other violence-encouraging risk factors. Those who frequently consume violent media are about

10% more likely to aggress (Gentile, 2003). That does not sound like much, but when one considers the implications of that increased risk across millions of people, it adds up to a great deal of harm, as small differences add up in large populations. With regard to sexualized violence and disrespect toward women often seen in many pornographic narratives, the increased risk of sexual violence in those who have other risk factors is even greater, and not surprisingly, it also increases the willingness to sexually objectify women even for those who do not aggress (Peter & Valkenburg, 2007).

It is hard to imagine a day when violent media will be a thing of the past. However, as with all of the fictions I discuss in these pages, we can mitigate its negative effects by becoming aware of and able to be critical of the stories that are being told to us. A group of researchers demonstrated how education can protect children as young as eight from adopting violent narratives by developing media literacy. They asked the children to identify low-probability outcomes in stories, such as a hero being shot at by many people but never being hurt, and alternative paths to conflict resolution (how else could the characters have solved the problem without violence?), as the most dangerous forms of media violence include a justification for it and the message that it is effective in reaching one's goals. Once they underwent this training, girls started to watch fewer violent programs. The amount of time boys spent viewing these stories did not change, but they got into fewer fights in school and were less likely to defy their teachers, thus the training appears to have had the effect of inoculating them against destructive behavior (Rosenkoetter et al., 2004).

## Conclusion

Sexism is the attitude that dehumanizes and devalues women. It distances men from empathizing with women and leads to the condoning and committing of physical and interpersonal violence against them. There is a cultural pressure for men to adopt this attitude, and as I have said many times before, it is very difficult to resist a pressure that one cannot name. In this chapter, I have tried to help people better understand this pressure and hopefully put the reader into a position to resist it and encourage others to do so as well. It would be naïve of me to suggest that everyday individual conversations will change the world all by themselves. We need real change in social-structural conditions that gave rise to these problems in the first place, and as I noted earlier, these conditions are ongoing as well as evolving. As the gendered division of labor slowly becomes a non-division of labor, we are seeing the development of the kinds of larger forces that reduce the prejudices of both sexes, as men and women are increasingly cooperating in the work that they do both at home and within the paid labor force. I wish I could say that this evolution will be complete within our short lifetimes, but despite its low likelihood, I firmly believe that we are heading in the right direction, albeit with many setbacks, toward ending sexism and its most toxic by-product, violence.

# 7

# THE LAST ACTION HERO

## The fiction of masculine mystique

I want to start by being clear that the enterprise of taking critical views of masculinity entails looking through a feminist lens in which gender is seen as socially constructed and therefore changeable. Many times when I offer gendered critiques, people react by saying that I am trying to dismantle masculinity itself, and because many believe the myth that feminism is men's enemy, even questioning the way we see men (and women) is often viewed as dangerous, as in the title of a recent book, *The End of Men (and The Rise of Women)* (Rosin, 2012).

I am not trying to dismantle masculinity; I am trying to help people understand it as a social pressure that sometimes facilitates and sometimes hampers people in gaining access to useful resources with which to live their lives. In taking a similar position, Liz Plank (2019a) explains, "This isn't an attack on gender; it is an improvement on it. This isn't an attack on personal freedom; it is an extension of it." (p. 290). I am also trying to help people understand that cultural conceptions of masculinity have the potential to affect those around us in both positive and negative ways. In recent years, there has been a good deal of discourse about so-called "positive masculinity" (see Hammer & Good, 2010; and Englar-Carlson & Kiselica, 2013). The more extreme advocates of this position (who do not include the scholars I just cited) seem uneasy with the idea that gendered critiques and ensuing cultural changes will result in a loss of some of the most beneficial aspects of the traditional masculine role: task completion, independence, risk taking, providing for one's family, loyalty, and courage, among others.

I observed this uneasiness most strikingly as a member of the Division for the Scientific Study of Men and Masculinity of the American Psychological Association. In 2007, I was the President-elect of this organization when, at Virginia Tech University, Seung-Hui Cho murdered 32 people and then committed suicide. In the aftermath of this tragedy, then-President Mark Stevens suggested that our division issue a statement about men and violence. I wrote the draft of the statement, which included the two facts I began with in Chapter 6: that although most men are not violent, most violent people are men. When I submitted the draft to the division's Board, several members expressed the opinion that it was "too negative." It was difficult for me to understand how we could put a positive perspective on 33 preventable deaths.

I am still a member of this association, which although it is open to all psychologists, is dominated by Clinical and Counseling Psychologists—those trained to treat people for mental health conditions and problems in living—and has many fewer psychologists of other specialties such as social, physiological, neuroscience, and developmental psychologies. Many of these therapists' interest in men and masculinity begins and ends with the male clients who come to their offices for help. Many are much less interested in social justice issues and therefore often take the position that in its official statements, the division should never say anything negative about men.

I take the position that although some stereotypical masculine characteristics have been historically associated with being a man, they do not need to be so. If these things are positive, then they should be positive regardless of what sex one is. And importantly, nearly all these entities are abstractions, which we can "unpack" by exploring the meanings of each. As you will see, far from dismantling traditional masculinity, I seek to criticize distortions of these abstractions and to expand them to help men embrace them in the right context. Returning to the metaphor I used in the preface of this book, I believe it would be beneficial to all if we are able to change the rigid boundaries of the "man box" into a semi-permeable membrane and not limit what is positive within the box to only men.

An abstraction is an idea that lacks a concrete and tangible nature; it stands apart from specific instances in the real world but can be applied to them (yourdictionary.com, 2020). Some examples are love, honesty, freedom, generosity, charity, determination, and trust. My experience is that people rarely try to explore how these abstract ideas translate into real-world actions. For instance, if someone says, "I love you" for the first time, it is considered very bad form to respond with, "What *exactly* do you mean by that?" As I did in an earlier work (Kilmartin & Berkowitz, 2005), I will take some abstractions that are traditionally associated with masculinity, give examples of how these ideas may become distorted, and offer ways of expanding these positive qualities for the benefit of self and/or others.

*Loyalty* entails feelings of support and commitment to another person or group. It tends to be a strong value in men's groups such as fraternities and athletic teams. But what often passes for loyalty is actually conformity. Take the instance where a friend, teammate, or fraternity brother is behaving self-destructively or being disrespectful. Others may think that they are being loyal by not challenging him, when in actuality, failing to do so can lead to bad situations. In this case, the sense of loyalty is distorted into "anything my buddy does is okay with me; I will always back him up." But if your buddy drinks 12 beers and then attempts to get behind the wheel of a car, is it loyal to not try to stop him? Because this action could result in harm—even death—then not intervening would seem to be remarkably *dis*loyal. If you care deeply about him, you will do what you can to help him stay safe. The easiest part about being a friend is to go along with something the friend is doing with which you agree. The most difficult part is trying to help lead the friend away from destructiveness, even when doing so may bring discomfort to one or both of you. Thus, we can expand the practice of loyalty to doing the hard work of making your organization or group more respectful and safer, which may include tolerating a good deal of interpersonal tension.

A quick story from my college years to illustrate the difference between loyalty and conformity: when I was in my third year, I became friends with a first-year student named Steve. Our nickname for him was Captain America, because he seemed to have it all. He was bright (he achieved a perfect grade point average in his first semester), handsome, funny, socially adept, and athletic (he had received but turned down college basketball scholarships). Early in the Spring semester, he discovered alcohol and as it turns out, did not handle it well at all. His drinking became out of control, and although I and several other friends noticed it, none of us said anything. He failed all his classes that semester, did not return the following year, and I never saw him again. I thought that I was being his friend by smiling every time he told me another story about his extreme substance abuse, but if I had been a truly loyal friend, I would have expressed concern about it and tried to see if I could help. Had I done so, he might have become angry or defensive, but the most difficult part of being a friend is in delivering unwelcome news when you think your friend could benefit from hearing it.

People who cultivate the habit of doing this difficult work are termed *tempered radicals*. They are those who are fully dedicated to the goals of their group or organization (Meyerson & Tompkins, 2007). So dedicated, in fact, that they are willing to challenge others within the group when they see that something is amiss, thus they can act as a catalyst for positive change within the group. But challenge usually meets with resistance, and tempered radicals sometimes put themselves at risk because they cause others to be uncomfortable, especially if they occupy positions at low levels of power within their group. To be a tempered radical, one must have the ability to be critical of the ways that the group operates. In other words, they cannot be so fully imbedded within the group culture that they are unaware of its negative aspects. Thus, they are able and willing to challenge the accepted assumptions of the group. For example, the president of a fraternity might engage an expert on sexual assault and dating violence to educate the fraternity members and/or to begin a mentorship program where older members teach younger ones about the importance of respect for all. Or a team athlete can interrupt stereotypical anti-feminine statements by his teammates. A corporation employee can advocate for more effective sexual harassment prevention and response within their company. In my opinion, tempered radicals are much more loyal to the group than conformists who take the stand that any criticism of the group is unwelcome and believe that such criticism signifies the radical's lack of dedication.

*Independence* is a quality often associated with being a man. It roughly means the ability to live one's life without being influenced or helped by others. Sometimes *counterdependence* or *oppositionalism* become disguised as independence. Fearing that they might be labeled as dependent, which is seen as a feminine quality, some men stubbornly resist anyone's suggestions for no useful reason. I have often seen it in my male students who refuse to ask for help, come to class, or complete assignments on time. As a result, they sabotage their own performances and are left feeling quite isolated. The refusal to ask for help is linked to a number of difficulties, the most extreme of which is a suicide rate roughly four times that of women (Addis & Mahalik, 2003). But men can be truly independent by making conscious decisions to do what they want and value even if others might consider doing so unmasculine. In challenging conformity, the tempered radical I described earlier is also acting independently.

*Courage* is taking a risk because one is committed to a valued outcome. Many men think of courage only in physical terms like running into a burning building, which is courageous (assuming that someone is *in* the building). Sometimes people mistake *bravado* for courage. Case in point: have you ever seen the Running of the Bulls in Pamplona, Spain? For my money, participating in it is one of the stupidest things that a human being can do—getting liquored up and running down slick cobblestone streets in front of stampeding tons of angry pot roast. The vast majority of participants are men and a few actually die in the process. Bravado is risk taking born of fear: if I risk my life, then hopefully nobody will question whether or not I am self-assured and tough. True courage involves a commitment to a cherished value, not merely taking a risk for its own sake. Again, we can interpret the tempered radical's actions as courageous. One can lose a job, friends, or other cherished things by taking an unpopular position.

Once I was giving a presentation and mentioned the Running of the Bulls and how stupid I thought it was, and an audience member remarked that he had, in fact, done it. I said to him, "Let me be clear that I am not calling you stupid. But I am saying that you *did a stupid thing*, and haven't we all?" I am sure many readers are familiar with jokes about men that begin with, "Hold my beer. Watch this." To take a physical risk as an end in itself is to capitulate to a negative aspect of masculine social pressure.

We can expand the ideal of courage into the moral realm. Here are a few statements that I would consider courageous in certain contexts:

"No thanks. I don't want another drink. I've had enough."
"I don't want to go to the strip club; I don't want that to be a part of my life."
"I don't like the way that you talk about women; it bothers me."
"I like you. I'm glad you're my friend."

*Respect* is courteous regard and attention for others' feelings and experiences. Respect for women is often distorted into *chivalry*, a set of rules for behaving in the company of women, such as refraining from profanity, helping women get seated or holding doors open for them, giving up one's seat on a crowded bus or train, filling a wine glass for a woman at a social occasion, and paying the restaurant bill when on a date. Peter Glick (2005) described most of these behaviors as "trivial niceties," that, although they are often appreciated, send two messages: first, that women are special and praiseworthy, and second, that they cannot get along without men's help. For instance, women who accept the chivalric rules may spend a lot of time at a party staring wistfully into the bottom of her empty wine glass in the hopes that some gentleman will notice and fill it for her. It may sound romantic, but at the same time, she is dependent on men if she wants another glass of wine.

True respect, however, is much more difficult than merely following gentlemanly etiquette. I ask my students, "Do you think that I have respect for you?," and they nearly all respond in the affirmative. Then I follow up with, "How do you know?," to which they often respond, "You ask us for our opinions," "You listen to us," "You work with us to make decisions about the class." Respect involves getting to know someone, listening to their voice, taking their feelings into account, negotiating decisions, and disagreeing without being disagreeable. Chivalry is rather easy; all one has to do is to learn the rules and follow them.

A few examples of the difference between chivalry and respect: a reader wrote to the advice columnist Carolyn Hax (2009) expressing frustration with her husband, who was quite a bit older than her. When they attended parties, he would nearly always want to go home before her, as he was introverted, and for him, parties can become overstimulating quite easily. On the other hand, she was an extrovert and very much enjoyed being around lots of other people. When he tells her that he would like to leave, she suggests that she stay at the party and get a ride home later from a good friend who was also in attendance. He found this arrangement unacceptable (as he also viewed her going to the party without him) because he believed in the "old school" chivalric dictate that a gentleman never leaves a lady unescorted in a social situation. And so, she can either decide to leave before she wants to, convince him to stay longer (which puts him in a bad mood), or insist that he defy the rule, which puts him in an even worse mood. He would not negotiate, his rationale being "that's just the way I was raised."

The fact that she was raised to be an independent woman who did not need a man's protection in social situations did not matter to him, and so what was on its face an expression of respect was really a means of his dominance and a communication that women are helpless without men. In fact, she felt *disrespected* by his insistence. Thus, reliance on the rules of chivalry can be constraining on women's choices. As my grandmother told my sisters, "If you want to be *treated* like a lady, you are going to have to *act* like a lady." Well, what if she does not want to act like a lady, such as if she wants to express anger at something offensive or do work that is considered masculine? She either chooses to experience the veneer of respect that chivalry affords or blame herself for the hostility she receives for not cooperating with antiquated social rules.

How many times do we hear, "that's just the way I was raised," as a justification for behaviors and attitudes? Although I believe that it is important to respect people's backgrounds and cultures, I do not think that they should stand alone in foreclosing discussion and disagreement. Ask yourself if there are ways in which you were raised that, as you grew into adulthood, you came to disagree with? Perhaps family members expressed racist, sexist, classist, or homophobic views, or told you that you should not associate with some people merely because of the social status they occupied.

A non-gendered example: for reasons that are unclear to me, I really do not like being called "sir;" perhaps because it makes me feel old. So, when someone says, "good morning, sir," I often respond with, "You don't have to call me sir," to which they sometimes reply, "Oh, yes I do sir; it's just the way I was raised." I feel like saying, "Oh, so it's all about *you!*" If calling me sir is intended as an expression of respect and I tell you that I don't receive it as such, you would do well to take my feelings into consideration. By the way, I do not make a big issue out of challenging this social convention, especially since I have done a good deal of work with the military, who can get into a lot of trouble for addressing someone in power without saying "sir" or "ma'am." My respect for them gives me empathy for the rigid conventions they are required to follow.

One evening, my wife and I went to a restaurant and our table was not yet ready, so we went to the bar, which was quite crowded, and ordered a drink while we waited, standing because no seats were available. A young man seated at the bar with his back to us turned around and saw that my wife was standing and so he asked her if she would like his seat. We had just driven an hour to get to the restaurant and she actually found standing to be refreshing after sitting for a while, and so she thanked him and politely declined. He turned back around and then after a few seconds said, "I would like you to sit," which left her with the decision of either having to be more insistent or politely taking his seat. To me, this was a good illustration of how sometimes chivalric behaviors are more directed toward the man's self-image of gallantry than they are toward expressing respect. After all, he had already asked about her preference and she had given it to him. She did, in fact, take the seat. I wonder if he would have become angry had she refused.

Peter Glick and Susan Fiske (2001) published an extensive and impressive piece of research on the relationship between benevolent and hostile sexism across many different countries with more than 15,000 participants. They termed benevolent sexism the "women are wonderful effect." Roughly equivalent to chivalry, benevolent sexism is a set of attitudes that communicate that women are praiseworthy yet incompetent. Hostile sexism is outright antipathy for women, something we usually think of when we are asked to define and give examples of sexism. The researchers noted that benevolent sexism is generally reserved for women who cooperate with men's dominance. Women who do not, often those who express feminist points of view, are at risk for being on the receiving end of hostile sexism. Benevolent sexism is seductive, securing women's cooperation but sometimes at the expense of their autonomy.

An example of the link between these two forms of sexism: let's say a woman is walking toward a door in a public building and a man is three steps behind her. He rushes up until he is three steps ahead of her and, smiling, opens the door for her as he steps aside. She may or may not like this action. Let's say for the sake of argument that she does not, as she finds it patronizing, and without really thinking, she reacts by giving him a "dirty look."

What happens next? Is it likely that he might express anger to her for not appreciating his gallantry? He might even call her a derogatory name. There is the link; she did not cooperate with his benevolent sexism so now she receives the hostile sexism. But what if he merely says, "I was only trying to help"? If so, I suggest that she says, "I'm glad you want to help. Can you help with some pay equity, childcare, and gender-based violence?" If men truly want to help women, they will help to open bigger doors than just the ones on public buildings.

And several of my women students have reported this experience. They are walking toward a door when a man steps up to open it for her. She thanks him and, after walking through, steps to a second set of interior doors. Because she arrives there before him, she opens the door for him, but he refuses to walk through before her. To me, this asymmetry reflects his discomfort with accepting help from a woman, the very thing he expects from her when he offers the same.

I want to be clear that within heterosexual relationships, conventions that appear chivalric are not wrong, only that they need not be applied in across-the-board fashion to dictate what all men should do for all women, since women are all different and want different things. For instance, I observed this scene many times from a couple who lived across the street from us. They would arrive in their car and park in front of their house. He would get out of the driver's seat (I never saw her driving) and she would wait patiently as he made his way around the car to open the passenger door for her. They both seemed to like this arrangement and if it works for them, I would never suggest that they should not do it. But in my relationship, it would seem ludicrous to both of us. A parallel: on Valentine's Day, one should not bring flowers to someone who is allergic to them.

Sexism operates quite differently from other forms of prejudice such as racism, religious intolerance, or homophobia because women and men are so interdependent (Rudman & Glick, 2008). As Glick (2005) pointed out, "If you hate black people, you probably don't hang out with them on the weekend." But if you hold prejudices toward women, you are likely married to one, have a mother and perhaps a daughter, and need to have cooperative relationships with women in a variety of settings. Benevolent sexism is thus necessary to maintain men's dominance. As Laurie Rudman and Peter Glick (2008) wrote regarding the sexes, "No other two groups have experienced such persistent differences in power and status coupled with such deep and intimate interdependence" (p. xi). In fact, men report that they like women more than they do men, but they also believe that women are less competent than men.

My presentation on this subject is titled, "Is Chivalry Dead? (I Hope So)." Because many people hold positive views of chivalry, they sometimes expect that I will be suggesting that men treat women even worse than many of them already do. I argue for nothing of the kind. While I suggest that we dismantle chivalry, I also argue that it can and should be transformed from trivial rule compliance into true respect.

To be clear, I am all for courtesy, consideration, and helpfulness. We can think of these entities as manifesting themselves as things that men do for women, or, as I propose, we can take it out of the gender schematic realm. As Sandra Bem (1993) noted, many other conceptualizations are possible that do not appeal to gender. To cite examples: should I, a middle-aged man, get up on a crowded bus to offer a fit, young woman my seat? Should a fit, young woman get up to offer her seat to a father with a baby in his arms? Once we move it out of the gender schema, we can envision a world where people are helpful and courteous to others regardless of the sex of the person who is the object of the behavior. Thus, I would do well on an airplane to help a person who is not as tall as I am to store their bag in an overhead bin regardless of whether that person is a woman or a man.

My colleague Terri tells of an experience she had after returning her rental car and waiting for a shuttle bus to the airport terminal. She was one of seven people waiting, the only woman in the group, and a good deal younger than any of the men, one of whom seemed quite old and walked with a cane. When the bus arrived, the driver came out and, without asking, picked up Terri's bag and placed it on the bus. He assumed that the men, including the one who walked with a cane, needed no help and that Terri did, despite the fact that she is quite tall, strong, and fit. Had the driver not seen the situation in gender schematic terms, he surely would have started with the older man who used a cane.

It is clear to me that men of conscience would do well to investigate the assumptions that they have internalized about being a man and do all that they can to communicate respect for people in all their actions. I have seen these assumptions play out in my sexual assault prevention work. The first topic, which I call "sexual assault prevention 101" is sexual consent. What I learned as a teenage boy, and what many teenage boys today learn, is that if you like a girl or woman, you try to kiss her, and hopefully they kiss you as well. After a while, you touch her breasts and if she says no or pushes your hand away, that means try again later. But if you touch someone sexually against their will, you have committed a crime, and so men and boys need to learn that being respectful to women and girls means securing their consent before you undertake the behavior rather than trying something and seeing if is okay, and you need to have consent for each new behavior. Perhaps she wants to kiss you but does not want to do anything else. One cannot assume that kissing implies consent for other things, nor that her previous willingness to engage in a behavior means that she will consent in the future. You may think back to a relationship you had in the past that did not end well. That is probably the last person you would consent to being sexual with, even though you had been before.

The best way to obtain consent is verbally. As my friend and colleague Mark Stevens humorously puts it, "When it comes to sex, use your mouth." I once asked a group of football players how they know when someone wants to kiss them. They respond with things like, "You look at her and she looks at you," "You lean in closer," and "Well ... you *just know*." I follow up with, "Have you ever been wrong?," and many acknowledge that in fact they have. "So," I ask, "what about saying, 'I'd really like to kiss you?'" At that point everyone including me seemed to notice the discomfort in the room.

But when you talk with many, although not all, women, they say that they would find asking if they want to kiss to be quite attractive because the man cared enough to make sure that it is what she wants, and that they might be more likely to say yes. But some women who follow sexual scripts that they have learned from media and elsewhere say things akin to, "I don't want him to ask; I want him to *take me*." But what does it feel like to be "taken" when you do not want to be? Awkward at best, traumatic at worst. Some men say that they do not ask because she might refuse, so they would rather be offensive than risk direct rejection.

I had this conversation with my Psychology of Men class every semester, and the following week a student followed up at the beginning of class, when I usually invite them to bring up any topic relevant to the course. She said, "Last week when we talked about asking to kiss, I was one of the ones who said I didn't want him to, but this weekend I went out with a guy and really did not like him. At the end of the evening, he tried to kiss me and it felt horrible. So now I've done a complete 'one-eighty,' I want them to ask every time."

Another frequent topic is the role of alcohol. People bring up the following question quite often: "What if both people are drunk? Did they assault each other?" The answer is deceptively simple: you are responsible for what you do when you drink. If you get drunk, drive, and cause an accident, you are held accountable for the damage you did. However, you are not responsible for what is done *to* you when you drink. If I go to a party and get falling-down drunk, it is my fault. But if, when I am passed out, someone steals my wallet or shaves off one of my eyebrows, that is their fault.

Then I ask, "Who is responsible for obtaining consent in a heterosexual situation?," and typically people either answer "the man," or "both people." But the correct answer is that the responsibility lies with whichever person wants to escalate the sexual activity. Because of cultural sexual scripts, that is often the man, but not always. If you want someone to be sexual with you, it is incumbent upon you to make sure that they want the same thing that you do. As my friend and colleague Gail Stern (2010) says, "that's just good customer service."

Several years ago, a student was referred to me because he had been found to be in violation of our university's sexual assault policy. He had not committed rape; if he had he would have been expelled. But he did touch someone sexually and against their will. As a consequence, he was required to meet with me, learn about the issues, and write an extensive paper about the topic. I told him that, if I had done something so disrespectful, I would want to do a lot of soul searching to figure out how and why I thought that my behavior was acceptable. In reaction, he threw up his hands, palms up, and said, "Hey, I'm just not going to drink and be around women ever again."

His response was indicative of the all-too-common belief that alcohol causes sexual assault. It is a very good thing that it does not, because, considering how many people drink, assaults would be many times more common than they already are. This assumption places the responsibility of the violence outside of the self, as if a foreign substance came into the body and caused the person to lose their mind. If the alcohol is to blame, then he can maintain the belief that he is a good person and that all he really needs to do is to be more careful about his drinking.

Many times in sexual assault situations, one or both people have been drinking, so it is important to discuss the role of alcohol. It is not causing the assault; the effect is akin to throwing gasoline on a fire. It may make the assault more likely because the offender drops their inhibitions and/or it helps to subdue the victim. Thankfully, most men who drink never commit an assault, so the alcohol only makes it more likely if the person has other violence-encouraging risk factors, as I wrote in Chapter 6.

When I talk to audiences about the role of alcohol, I always acknowledge that I like to drink and that the responsible use of alcohol is not a problem. And so, I make it clear that I am not giving a temperance lecture; to do so would be hypocritical. Sometimes I underscore that point by saying that I am here to tell them that they should not blame drinking for assault—that alcohol can be a beautiful thing. I also make it clear that those of us who enjoy alcohol should never pressure those who do not want to drink to join us.

But there are good reasons to drink and bad reasons to drink. A good reason is that I like the taste of the drinks and the social interaction that goes with it. A bad reason to drink is that the person to my immediate left just bounced a quarter into a cup. So, although I am supportive of responsible drinking, I am adamantly opposed to drinking *games*. I ask the audience what they are designed to do, and pretty much everyone knows the answer: to have people drink more than they initially intended to. In these games, rather than taking a drink because you want to, you take it on a schedule that has been established by the social pressure of the rules of the game. Thus, the game largely takes away your ability to consent to put something into your body. I hope that you can see the parallel with sexual consent. And, to me, the best thing about drinking socially is getting to know other people and having pleasant interactions. But if you turn the social activity into a sport, you engage in much less actual conversation.

I was once asked to act as an advocate for a student bringing a sexual assault complaint against another student in a student conduct hearing. I was amazed that one of the panelists asked numerous questions about the complainant's drinking on the night in question. It soon became clear to me that if it was established that she was drunk, he would attribute at least part of the responsibility for the attack to her. This was a specific instance of the pervasive problem of victim blaming. People often work backwards from the attack, find something that the victim did that made her more vulnerable (such as drinking a lot, accepting a ride from a stranger, or going to someone's room, etc.) and attribute the violence to that mistake that the victim made. Victim blaming is a psychological security operation. If I can find something the victim did and believe that it caused the attack, I am safe if I do not do that thing, or for victims themselves, I am safe if I do not do that thing *again*.

My friend and colleague Gail Stern (2010), whom I mentioned earlier, is a terrific trainer who helps people empathize with rather than blame the victim. She asks, "When you see a teenage horror movie, how do you know that someone is about to be attacked?," and people answer, "The music." Then she says, "Wouldn't it be great if there were music in real life? Or have you ever been in a situation where *you* can hear the music but the other person seems not to?" We expect victims to have seen into the future and hold them to a standard to which we do not hold ourselves. Ask yourself if you have ever misjudged someone else's character or made a wrong assessment of a situation. You are likely not friends with everyone with whom you have ever been friends, and being sexually assaulted is not a fitting consequence for making mistakes. The full responsibility for an assault rests with the assailant, regardless of how easy or difficult a target the victim was.

Another question I frequently hear in my work as a sexual assault prevention educator is, "How many beers can a woman have before it becomes illegal to have sex with her?" Legally, there is no specific answer to this question, as it depends on many factors such as her size, how fast she is drinking, what her tolerance level is, whether she's had something to eat, etc. But the "how many beers" question is really a coded question. What is really being asked is, "What is the maximum amount of manipulation that I can bring to bear on a person before I am held legally accountable?" I do not think that this is the standard we want to set, and we do not think of applying the minimum standard in other areas of our lives. For instance, I do not think that any college student has as their goal to graduate with a 2.00 grade point average and exit the workforce at the same level in which they enter.

Picture a continuum with "fully respectful" on one end and "fully disrespectful" on the other. Somewhere near the latter pole the law or an organizational policy draws a line and says that anything to the disrespectful side of the line is illegal or against policy. I do not want, nor do I expect, men to be just short of that line. I believe that all people are capable of fully respectful relationships and interactions. The true "male bashers" are those who think that men are not capable of such.

One April the campus police at my university, in a well-meaning but misguided gesture, put up a sign for Sexual Assault Awareness month that read, "Real men don't rape." Do we really want to "set the bar" at "don't rape" for young college men, who are supposed to be among the best and the brightest? Too many men believe that their participation in violence prevention is merely to refrain from criminal behavior. When I talk to men, I help them to understand we need more from them than to not break the law. Moreover, the phrase "real men" is used to shame men into behaving in line with expectations by threatening to unsex them if they do not. Many men were justifiably insulted by this message.

At the end of my session with the football players in which I suggested that they appropriately and verbally ask for consent, one of them said, "Are you nuts? Talk to a woman before having sex with her? I couldn't possibly do that." So, I asked him what position he played and he said that he was a cornerback. This is the defensive player whose main task is to cover pass receivers. Because they cannot know where the pass receiver is going to go, they must watch them, and so they run at full speed nearly every play, but backwards. I asked him if running backwards at full speed felt natural and normal the first time he tried it and he said, "Of course not. It felt really awkward." "So why," I asked, "did you spend so much time learning to do this crazy thing?" The answer was obvious: because he wanted to be a good football player. Yes—we expend time and energy in learning a skill when we value the outcome, so if you want to be a more respectful person, you will expend the effort.

It is my firm belief that leading an intentional life involves understanding the social pressures placed upon us, one of which is gendered expectations. And it is my firm value that the effort is well worth the cost. The final chapter of this book contains suggestions around how one might begin this exploration.

# 8

# ONWARD THROUGH THE FOG

## The future of masculinities

Given our understanding of the forces that shape culture, we can forecast the future of gender arrangements. Holding on to "traditional" conceptions about the sexes has predictable consequences. However, when men become critical of the stories that are being told to them and when they substitute reality for fiction, they gain a new language with which to understand their worlds. Doing so puts them into a position to make informed choices about their behavior rather than merely "going along with the program." Or in other words, it is difficult to follow something other than the program when one does not know what the program is. I have often put it this way in presentations on the topic—so often, in fact, that it has become something of a mantra for me: it is very difficult to resist a pressure that one *cannot name*.

One of my intellectual heroes is the great developmental psychologist Sandra Bem (1993), the inventor of Gender Schema Theory, which I also discussed in Chapters 2 and 7 and return to here as we explore the possibilities to acquire more accuracy in our judgments. Bem theorized that, because children are "sophisticated pattern-seeking organisms," early in their lives they begin to put things and experiences into categories to make sense of their worlds. For instance, when children begin to learn how to talk, they not only acquire increasingly larger vocabularies, they also learn the deep structure of the language. We know this from the mistakes they make, which linguists call "overregularizations"—the application of grammatical rules in places where there are grammatical exceptions. For instance, most verbs form a past tense by adding the letters "ed" to the end (play to played, walk to walked, progress to progressed, etc.). But many verbs do not follow this pattern: go, take, wear, tear, write, and many others. It is not unusual to hear a child say something like "I goed there," or "you teared the paper," which indicates that they know the rule for past tense (usually without being explicitly taught it) but have applied it incorrectly to an exceptional situation because they discovered the patterns from their experiences with language. In fact, they start to do so before they even utter a word, learning the language receptively from hearing others while the parts of the brain that are responsible for productive speech develop (Eliot, 2009). Pattern seeking seems to be innate because it has great survival value, for instance in helping animals (including us) to find food, keep safe, and communicate.

Likewise, children learn gender categories from extracting patterns they experience when "exposed to a culturally-relevant social practice." For instance, noticing that when an adult is pushing a stroller, it is much more often a woman, or when someone is building a house, it is more often a man. And as they do with language, they overgeneralize and form gender categories when other categories are quite possible, such as that, when an adult is pushing a stroller, it is much more often a parent than a non-parent, and when someone is building a house, it is more often a paid laborer than a white-collar worker. Gender schema are so ingrained that there is a story of a mother asking her young daughter what she wanted to be when she grew up and the daughter said, "a nurse." The mother asked, "Why not a become a doctor?," to which the daughter replied, "No—girls aren't doctors," despite the fact that her mother was a doctor!

Another case in point which I mentioned briefly in Chapter 2: when I was teaching at the US Air Force Academy, two of my cadet students who are women went out to dinner at a local restaurant wearing civilian clothes, and before the bill came they asked the server if the restaurant offered a military discount. The server replied, "Yes, but only for active-duty military, not for military spouses." Clearly it did not occur to the server that the military has many active-duty women.

These overgeneralizations can be overcome when people learn alternative cosmologies. For instance, once my students informed the server that they were, in fact, active-duty military, the server might have been less likely to make an error like this in the future. The "gender schema" as Bem called it, is only one possibility among many, and people can learn how to form more accurate and more sophisticated categorizations. For example, Bem offers an "individual difference schema." Instead of believing that "men are aggressive," one could believe that "some people are more aggressive than others; some aggressive people are men and some are women." For the server in the restaurant scenario, the gendered schema "man/woman" could be replaced with the more accurate "military/non-military."

Many gender studies instructors use the following riddle I alluded to earlier to illustrate the ubiquity of gender schema: a boy and his father are riding in a car together and they suffer a terrible accident. The father is killed and the son, badly injured, is transported to the hospital to undergo surgery. The surgeon enters and says, "I cannot operate on this boy; he is my son." But we just said that the father was killed so how can this be? The answer, as you may recall, is that the surgeon is the boy's mother. The riddle is difficult for many because they have unconsciously associated surgeons with men.

Bem referred to gender beliefs as "the default options" in a culture: the patterns most people abstract because we live in a culture that puts gender into all kinds of places where it need not belong: colors, preferred foods and drink, ways of talking, mannerisms, etc. I took Bem's language of default options and, using my limited knowledge of computers, where the term *default* is most often used, constructed an analogous model for how individuals and cultures can change.

When you start your computer, a number of things happen that are left in place by doing nothing; these are the defaults set by those who designed the equipment. For instance, the icons that appear on the screen are of a standard size: about one square inch on most desktop computers. You can change the size of those icons (when I mention this to audiences, the younger people look at me as if to say, "Duh!" and the older people's eyes widen as if to say, "You CAN?!").

Changing a default like the size of your screen icons requires three things. The first is knowledge: you need to know that it is possible to change the default or obviously the size of the icons would remain the same unless you made a remarkable series of random errors that accidentally altered them. The second is motivation: maybe you know that icon size can change, but maybe they function fine for you just the way they are, and so you are not motivated to reset the default. But maybe you do not see very well and it would be better for you if they were larger, or maybe you simply do not want your desktop to look like everyone else's, in which case it is a fashion choice to change icon size. The third is skill: if you know about the default and want to change it, you will have to learn how to do so. Or to put it another way, change comes when you know, care, and act.

And so it is with gender, the cultural pressure to behave and experience the self in concert with the social expectations placed on people whose bodies are generally interpreted as belonging to one sex or another. The first condition, knowledge, has the potential to set change in motion. If I know what I have been led to believe by the culture—the gendered fictions—then once I name the social pressures, I can decide if I want to resist them and in what circumstances I want to do so, and then if I do, I must learn how to activate that resistance. Under what circumstances might it be beneficial to resist gendered pressure? I can think of at least two: if conformity conflicts with a person's goals or values and/or if conformity results in harm to the self or others. Recall from Chapter 4 the story about Ryan learning to confront his friends by refusing to go to a strip club. He did so because he believed that those businesses were exploitive and thus they offended his value of fairness. Or a man who steps in to interrupt the mistreatment of another person and does so to prevent harm. Or a man who decides to seek psychotherapy because he is depressed and has urges to harm himself.

As an educator, my task is to facilitate knowledge by exposing the defaults. It is not to tell people how to live their lives but to put them into position to make informed decisions. I endeavor in my work to be descriptive and not prescriptive. In that vein, I did a solo theatre performance entitled "Crimes Against Nature" (Kilmartin, 2020) for many years. It is mainly comprised of personal stories about, for example, my relationship with my father, how I learned about sex, and how I negotiated the pressure to be an athlete. (If you are interested in seeing it, look in the reference section and you will see a link to it on *Vimeo*—available for the low,

low, low price of … free.) A theme that runs throughout is that boys and men have feelings other than anger and lust and that it is generally healthy to be able to express these feelings when we want to. In the show, I use a shorthand description of men who blindly conform to gender stereotypes as "guys" rather than "men." After one performance, a young man approached me, upset and angry, and said something like this: "I felt like you were disrespecting me, telling me how to be. I *like* being a 'guy.' Go to work, come home, watch ESPN, eat buffalo wings; feelings are a nuisance."

My first reaction was, "It's a *play*! When you saw Romeo and Juliet, did you think that you were supposed to commit suicide if things didn't work out with your girlfriend?" I was being *de*scriptive—telling my stories in the hopes that audience members would revisit theirs. But this young man thought that I was being *pre*scriptive—saying that he should negotiate masculine social pressure in the same way that I do. I do not want to tell men how they should deal with the world, but I do want them to be informed of the repercussions of doing so in whatever way they choose. An excellent example is this young man's statement, "feelings are a nuisance."

In a similar vein, a woman once told me a story about a conversation she had with a male co-worker. She said to him, "I'm feeling really sad today and I don't know why." His response: "Well … stop it!" Boys and men are encouraged to deny the experience of nearly every kind of emotion (with the exception of anger and lust), and if one practices the suppression of feelings, many can become very adept at "stop it." But here is what can happen as a result: the experience of negative emotion and that of positive emotion are highly correlated—a "package deal." And so, if you become facile at suppressing negative feelings, over time you will lose your ability to experience positive ones. If you decide that you will never feel sad, anxious, worried, or disappointed, you will also lose your ability to experience joy, satisfaction, happiness, and gratitude. It is a Faustian "pact with the devil" that this young man was making without knowing it. I was not about to tell him how to live his life but I wanted him to know what price he was paying for choosing to do it in the way he did. James Nelson (1997) likens the suppression of feeling to the armor worn by medieval knights, saying "on the one hand, it protects us; on the other, it prevents us from leaping, dancing, and being seen."

The suppression of emotion also comes with other costs. At the extreme, it is manifested in the psychological condition known as *alexithymia* (Sifneos, 1972), which literally means "no words for feelings." People with this condition exhibit emotional numbness, almost as though they are sleepwalking through life. Alexithymic individuals, most of whom are men, show higher levels of heart rate reactivity, high blood pressure and other negative physiological effects (Smiler & Kilmartin, 2019). Moreover, alexithymia damages relationships because emotionality is often essential in being a partner, parent, or friend (Lynch & Kilmartin, 2013). Not surprisingly, alexithymia has a strong correlation with the acceptance of stereotypical masculinity (Levant, Hall, Williams, & Hasan, 2009) and is also associated with a low degree of willingness to seek medical or psychological help (Addis & Mahalik, 2003).

Three other cases in point—one quite unfortunate, one which had the potential to create problems, and the other downright tragic—to illustrate the negative consequences of failing to name, and thus to resist, negative masculine social pressure. The first is the story of a man named "Les."

My great friend Mitch, after 20 years of marriage, decided to get divorced. And so, he moved out of his house and into a spare room in his friend Les' house while he decided on and prepared to transition to a more permanent living situation. Les, then in his mid-40s, had lived alone for all his adult life. He is heterosexually identified and always thought that he would someday be a husband and father, but he has never been able to sustain a relationship with a woman that lasted more than a few weeks.

Why not? Our first guesses might be that perhaps there is something very undesirable about Les as a potential mate; that perhaps he is physically unattractive, alcoholic, cruel, or chronically unemployed, etc. But in fact, he is none of those. He has worked at a good job for decades, owns his home and is debt free. He drinks, perhaps a little too much at times, but he is not someone who gets falling-down drunk on a daily basis, and he does not become belligerent when he drinks. He has no history of being violent or otherwise abusive in relationships. And although he is not strikingly handsome, he is fit, and his physical attractiveness would make him more than acceptable to many heterosexual women.

So, what is getting in the way of Les' stated life goals of marrying and parenting? One does not even have to talk with him to find out. Just looking around his house, you can see that Les is a walking hypermasculine stereotype, a person whom the Roman poet Ovid referred to as a *puer aeturnus*, an eternal boy. Much later, psychoanalyst Carl Jung (1959/1989) suggested that the eternal boy was primordial in the form of what he called an archetype. On the positive side, this part of the psyche allows the person to be playful and dream. But overemphasizing it keeps the man from responding to the demands of being an adult.

Les' house has a pool table in the living room and nothing but sports posters on the wall. His refrigerator contains little more than beer. He owns an extensive pornography collection. He seems unable to talk about anything other than sports, sex, and sometimes his job as a salesperson. Occasionally Mitch tried to engage him in more serious conversations, once asking, "What kind of woman would you eventually like to have for a wife?"

To me, Les' answer encapsulated his difficulties. He responded, "Intelligent, but submissive." In other words, he wanted a mate who would give him new information and engage him in interesting conversations, but he did not want one with whom he would have to negotiate a relationship nor attend to her feelings when they disagreed (which, let's face it, is inevitable in relationships at least from time to time). I suppose that there are intelligent but submissive women out in the world but I am also guessing that they are rather difficult to find. Les did not want a partner; he wanted a helpmate and perhaps someone who would metaphorically "hold up the mirror" to him.

What appears to have happened is that Les has uncritically bought into a simplistic and hypertrophied version of masculinity, probably without even realizing it. And because he has, he is powerless to change in the direction of becoming an adult. In the process, he is failing to reach his important life goals of marriage and family. And here is my little joke: men do not have to settle for Les.

The second story was a problem one of my students related in class that has stayed with me for a very long time. Although she was not married, she lived with a man who was the father of their child, and so they had a family living arrangement. She said, "I want my boyfriend to help out around the house, but he can't seem to manage to cook frozen fish sticks and he always messes up the laundry." I immediately noticed the language she was using: "I want [him] to *help out*." If he is the helper, it seems that the household duties are seen as her responsibility and that his labor is seen by both of them as optional. I asked what kind of work he did, and she said that he was a carpenter. That means that he solves physical problems all day long, so why can he not figure out how to make fish sticks and do laundry?

Have you ever looked at the directions on a box of frozen fish sticks? One: preheat oven to 350 degrees. Two: *remove fish sticks from box*. They do not even assume that you know that you are not supposed to place a paper carton into a hot oven. I do all the laundry at my house and assuming that you have a modern washer and dryer, I can teach you everything you need to know about doing the laundry in about five minutes. There is nothing difficult about either of these tasks. They are certainly nothing compared to advanced carpentry skills.

My guess (it is a guess because I have never met this man) was that he did not want to do what in his father's and grandfathers' days would have been considered "women's work," and that he was either consciously feigning incompetence or unconsciously sabotaging his performance of these simple tasks. Once the sexual urgency in the relationship wears off, and if my student had the financial and emotional wherewithal to survive on her own, I think it is highly likely that she would leave the relationship, figuring that his presence created more work and less relationship satisfaction for her. It reminded me of old situation comedies where a standard plot was husband and wife trading lives for a couple of days and both finding that they were remarkably incompetent at the others' tasks, when in the real world, husbands/fathers are capable of learning every kind of domestic work as wives/mothers that does not require the production of breast milk.

In the idealized 1950s arrangement, the husband worked outside the home in the paid labor force and the wife was responsible for all the (unpaid) domestic labor. But such an arrangement is not feasible for most couples (and as I mentioned in Chapter 5, not even feasible for a sizeable proportion of the population even during that era), who need more than one source of income. If the deal is that the husband succeeds for the wife, who manages the household and parenting duties, once the wife is directly contributing financially, would it not seem fair that their domestic labor should also become more equal? In one study, 81% of relationships in which husbands were unwilling to negotiate a fair power arrangement in work and family labor with their wives resulted in a dissolution of the relationship (Gottman and Silver, 1999). For Les, the relationships were over almost before they started. For my student's boyfriend, I am not sure because I have not maintained contact with her, but I would not be surprised at all if by now they are no longer together.

The third and tragic story is one told to me by a former student named Erin, who in addition to being a full-time student also worked part-time as an emergency medical technician. She wrote in her class journal that, during one shift, the ambulance crew was dispatched to a rural part of a nearby county. The wife of a man we will refer to as Jake called 911 saying that she believed that he might be having a heart attack. The ambulance crew arrived to find Jake sweating (despite it not being warm), out of breath, and down on one knee, unable to stand. His wife and two young children were at his side, looking quite helpless. The ambulance crew chief told Jake that he might well be having a heart attack, that they needed to examine him, and that, if they ascertained that this was indeed the case, to transport him to the hospital as quickly as possible. Time is critically important during a cardiac event.

But Jake had the right to refuse treatment, and that is exactly what he did, saying, "I'm no sick person; real men don't go to the hospital." By the time there were a few other attempts to convince him to cooperate, his wife and children were crying and pleading with him, and Erin wrote that by this time, she was also pleading, "PLEASE let us help you." The crew chief told Jake that if, in fact, he was having a heart attack, that he would probably soon lose consciousness from lack of oxygen, and at that point, he would not be able to refuse treatment, as they would be required by law to take all possible measures to save the life of an unresponsive person. He continued to refuse and, in fact, became unconscious within a few minutes. The crew was on him right away, loaded him into the ambulance, and made their way to the hospital while they used a defibrillator on his heart. Jake was dead upon arrival to the hospital. He had squandered critical minutes because he was so beholden to his distorted vision of what it means to be a man that he might well have paid for it with his life.

## Men and physical health

I was first exposed to the study of men and masculinities as a graduate student. At the time, there was very little research in the area and the first thing that got my attention, and that continues to astound me, is the fact that men's average life expectancy is significantly shorter than women's, a difference known as the *mortality gap*.

How large is the discrepancy between men's and women's average longevities? It depends on several factors. At the time when I first began to read about it, the difference between US men and women was around 7 years. More recently, it has decreased to about 5.5. In Russia, it is around 13 years! And there are racial discrepancies as well; minority men tend to not live as long as White men but also do not live as long as minority women. Males in the mostly White, affluent Washington, DC suburban Fairfax County, Virginia have the longest life expectancy for men anywhere in the US. A scant few miles across the Potomac River in

Southwest Washington, DC, the men have the second shortest lifespans in the country, likely because of some combination of poverty, racial discrimination, dangerous and/or stressful environments, and lack of access to health care.

What are the major causes of the mortality gap? Part of it can be attributed to biological factors such as testosterone's negative effects on cholesterol and estrogen's protective effect. But most of the gap is attributable to behavioral factors. Here is but a partial list of things men do more often than women that are associated with risk: refusing to wear sunscreen or seatbelts, smoking and/or drinking heavily, playing dangerous sports, engaging in violence, refusing to visit physicians, and working in hazardous environments. Men commit suicide about four times as often as women (Courtenay, 2011). During the Covid-19 pandemic in 2020, men were much less likely than women to safeguard their and others' health by wearing face masks, even though men were significantly more likely than women to die if they contracted the virus (Markus, 2020). This failure to engage in protective health behavior was especially pronounced in men who endorsed traditional masculine gender norms (Markus, 2020).

Once I learned about the behavioral aspects of the mortality gap, I realized that many male premature deaths are preventable if we can get men to live their lives differently. Not surprisingly, men who subscribe to stereotypical masculine ideologies are at a much higher risk than those who do not. For example, people (who are mostly men) who are chronically angry show a significantly increased risk for cerebrovascular accident (stroke) (Williams, et al., 2002). To me, the most astounding thing about the toxic side of masculinity is that it is *literally* killing us. As I write this, I am aware that by the time my father was my age, he had been dead for 15 years. Part of my passion for this subject is personal, as I believe that cultural masculine demands are at least partly responsible for my father's early death.

In what parts of the world is the mortality gap smallest? It might surprise some to learn that it is in countries such as Iceland, Switzerland, and Norway, where women's social and economic statuses are most comparable to those of men. Men in these countries also fare better in other measures of well-being, such as mental health and lower rates of divorce, suicide, and violence (Plank, 2019). In other words, feminism appears to be men's best friend. These data fly in the face of commonly held beliefs that feminists seek to disempower men. In fact, as I mentioned in Chapter 4, feminists as a group actually hold *higher* opinions of men than women who do not identify as feminists. People seem to not notice the facts that about 90% of adult feminists are (guess what?) married to men, and that many have sons whom they want to see living in a better world.

To engage in a social movement, one must believe two things: first, that the current system is unfair. Those who are comfortable with the social and economic dominance of men-as-a-group relative to women-as-a-group (as before, I use the hyphens to emphasize that these are aggregate differences; there are certainly individual women who are relatively powerful and individual men who are relatively powerless) would be very unlikely to engage in the social movement. If one sees the current situation as equitable, then why try to change it? Those who believe that disadvantaged people brought their problems on themselves and have the wherewithal to solve them are the least likely to do anything to help.

The second thing one must believe to engage in a social movement is that the current situation is unstable—that it is possible to change it. If we go back to the 1960s Civil Rights Movement in the United States, would people bother to organize bus boycotts, lunch counter sit-ins, and freedom rides if they thought that none of these things would make a difference? Obviously not. And so, feminists, although many are justifiably frustrated and angry with men, also have faith in us. They believe that we can do better. As I stated earlier, the real "male bashers" are those who believe that we must lower our expectations of men—that men are not capable of being kind, compassionate, self-caring, and thoughtful.

## How can men be allies in the struggle to end sexism?

Sexism is often portrayed as a "women's issue," but this and all forms of inequality are human issues, and the by-products of gendered inequality negatively affect women and men, in that order. People from dominant groups have important roles to play in the struggle for equality. We need those from dominant racial groups to exert efforts to decrease racism, wealthy people to help reduce economic inequality, heterosexual and cisgendered people to work against homophobia and transphobia, and men to do what they can to help end sexism. I wrote a recent chapter on the strategies and theories for encouraging men to be allies to women (Kilmartin, 2017) which I summarize below.

I begin by saying that there are forces that can both encourage men to participate and those that will make it less likely that they will do so. If there were no facilitators, nobody would get involved. If there were no barriers, everyone would be. Therefore, building a critical mass of men who are willing to work against sexist attitudes and practices means that we must enhance the factors that make it more likely that they will participate and decrease those that make it less likely.

What are the factors that help to get men involved? For me, the most important one is a sense of fairness, a belief that sexism is unjust and that it offends our egalitarian sensibilities. As I mentioned earlier in describing my own research, the majority of men hold favorable attitudes toward women and are bothered when women are mistreated. At the same time, most believe that they are unusual in this regard compared with most men. We can help them to understand that there are many like-minded men with the use of educational interventions such as the social norms approach I described earlier (Kilmartin et al., 2008). Second, we can invite them to join the cause by helping them understand that their efforts are needed in working toward social justice—that they have unique roles to fill. We can help them understand the simultaneous processes of continuity and change to help them gain an understanding that sexism is both unfair and unstable. We can find ways to support them through the frustrations of this sometimes difficult work. And we can teach them specific techniques that they can use to challenge sexism, building their confidence in their effectiveness as they practice these skills.

The following story is an illustration of an effective action by a male ally. A student at a small college was taking a summer class on the topic of health. The instructor had designated one class period in the middle of the summer session as "Body Fat Day." Students would be required to come to class in bathing suits that day and each would have their body fat measured and the result announced to the class. Several students seemed uncomfortable at this suggestion and one approached the instructor, told him so, and requested an alternative assignment. The instructor held fast to the requirement, saying that this exercise was the only way to learn about the topic and that if the student refused to participate, it would have a significantly negative effect on her grade.

Given the power difference between student and instructor and his unwillingness to negotiate the assignment, the student began to weigh her options and considered the following courses of action: (1) she could go through the exercise and tolerate the discomfort, but she found the idea so traumatizing that she feared a full-blown panic attack; (2) she could drop the course, which would result in delaying her timeline for graduation; (3) she could refuse to participate and absorb the negative effect on her grade; or (4) she could file a formal complaint of hostile learning environment sexual harassment with the college, which would require considerable time and effort. She found none of these four alternatives acceptable.

But fortunately, there was another possibility. She approached my friend and colleague Alan, from whom she had taken a course the previous semester, and whom she knew to be expert on gender issues and harassment. She explained her dilemma, and Alan asked her if she would feel comfortable with his meeting with the instructor and negotiating on her behalf. Alan was a tenured full professor, and so he had a level of power and status at least equal to, and probably greater than, the instructor. The student immediately and gratefully accepted the offer.

Alan approached his colleague as a collaborator, not an adversary. As it turns out, the health instructor was not a habitual and predatory harasser. If he were, there would probably be no other way to influence him than to file a formal complaint. But the instructor was a well-meaning person who was merely under-sensitive to students' experiences. Alan explained to him that students might be highly uncomfortable with Body Fat Day for many different reasons. They might have a history of being body-shamed or sexually abused. They might have a painful self-consciousness about their appearance. Or they might not want to appear in a bathing suit for religious reasons. In fact, Alan said, a student does not really need an explicit justification for wanting to opt out of the exercise. At a basic level of choice and autonomy, people should be able to decide the degree to which they are willing to have their bodies scrutinized. In fact, it had never occurred to the instructor to join the exercise by himself wearing a bathing suit to class.

Alan also told the instructor that should one or more of the students file a complaint, he would have to go through a long and difficult process of responding to the complaint. And even if there were no complaint, an assignment so problematic could have a significantly negative effect on his course evaluations and thus his career. This strategy was, as I discussed in Chapter 6, to appeal to enlightened self-interest. The instructor immediately understood that the event could create problems for all and so he canceled Body Fat Day. Alan helped him to construct a less intrusive activity, and the problem was solved.

## Prejudice reduction

One conceptualization of prejudice is a barrier to action; another is a facilitator. If we view prejudices, including sexism, narrowly as being merely consciously held attitudes, then all we need to do is to believe that the world ought to be fair and people should be treated with respect. In this case, the only work I engage in is on myself by striving to be a good person. But prejudice does not just exist in the minds of individuals; it takes place in the world in the forms of implicit biases and social practices that maintain an inequality of outcome for members of some groups compared with those of others. From this definition, the work expands into first, examining my own reactions that may be beneath the surface, second, listening to women's voices and experiences, and third, working to change sexist social systems.

Following are a few words about implicit bias, which is a well-documented phenomenon. Nearly all of us have prejudices that lurk beneath the surface of our consciousness (Kirwan Institute, 2020). The first step in working with implicit biases is to acknowledge that they exist. If you want to have a humbling experience, go to one of the many available on-line sites to take one of the many versions of the Implicit Associations Test (IAT) and you will likely find that you have prejudices of which you may have been unaware.

Implicit biases often play out in people who think of themselves as fair-minded by denying that they have biases and believing that the choices they make are based on other rationales, thus maintaining their positive self-concepts. For example, people in dominant groups will offer assistance to people in subordinated groups if they have no rationale not to do so. But they are less likely to help when they have an excuse such as that they did not have the time (Livingston, 2011). This kind of rationale seemed to be in play during the 2016 United States presidential election when many people stated that they had no problem voting for a woman but would not vote for Hillary Clinton, instead abstaining from the election, voting for a third-party candidate who had no chance to win, in effect a vote for her opponent, or even voting for her opponent, who would become the only US President who had no experience in government or the military.

But once you acknowledge implicit bias, then what? As one of my students so succinctly asked, "What can we do about it? You don't know what you don't know." The answer is that you need to go looking for it. As Carol Tavris and Elliot Aronson (2008) stated in their excellent work, *Mistakes Were Made, but not by Me: Why We Justify Foolish Beliefs, Bad Decisions, and Hurtful Acts*, "Drivers cannot avoid having blind spots in their field of vision, but good drivers are aware of them" (p. 44).

According to the research, prejudiced and less prejudiced people do not differ in *stereotype activation* (Fazio & Olson, 2003). Less prejudiced people work to recognize that activation by tuning in to their perceptions and feelings and then taking steps to counteract the stereotypes. If one practices enough, over time the stereotype activation itself decreases (Kawakami, et al., 2000). Thus, dealing with implicit bias is a set of skills that improve with practice (Schwartz, et al., 2016). We invest time and effort in learning a skill when we value the outcome enough to believe that it is worth our time (Kilmartin, 2017).

An illustration from my own experience: I am from the age cohort widely known as the "baby boomer" generation. When I was growing up, very few people had tattoos, and those who did were nearly all men. I did not see a woman with a tattoo until I was well into middle age. Even among the relatively few men who wore them, I do not recall seeing one anywhere but on the forearm when I was young. Today, of course, they are everywhere—on people of all ages and in many places on the body. When a student, especially a young woman, or anyone who has tattoos on their necks or all over their arms, walks into my classroom, my stereotype becomes activated. Without realizing it consciously, I say to myself, "Uh-oh. Here comes trouble." But after a while I tuned in to this reaction and learned to produce another voice that says, "Uh-oh. Did I just stereotype this person?" Then I take steps to try to make sure that my implicit biases against people with tattoos do not get in the way of my treating the student fairly. And as I repeated this practice, over time I noticed that I was not having nearly as much of a reaction when the heavily tattooed student walked in. And of course, I learned from interacting with people who have tattoos that they are all different and that very few fit the stereotypes that I learned as a child without even realizing it.

Another factor that gets in the way of men's involvement is the beliefs in antiquated gender stereotypes, the very ones I am trying to challenge throughout this book. Many of these are grounded in the definition of masculinity as anti-femininity, which, combined with male dominance in the society at large, fuels the devaluation of both stereotypically feminine behaviors and by extension, of women and girls themselves. I wrote earlier about many of these mistaken beliefs such as that the sexes are opposite or adversarial, and that women's gains must necessarily be accompanied by men's losses (zero-sum gender beliefs). To overcome this barrier, we have to challenge these assumptions and help men to see that joining women in the struggle to end sexism is not only the right thing to do, but that it may also enhance their own lives by helping them to break free of the more harmful aspects of masculine social pressure. For example, as I mentioned at the beginning of this book, many of the characteristics that are culturally defined as feminine are those that will help men to become better friends, fathers, and partners.

## Men working to end sexism

Some men dedicate their lives to the reduction of sexism and to doing other social justice work, but most will have other priorities. Still, even men who are not involved in career activism can be effective allies to women in their everyday lives by learning how to interrupt sexism and to intervene in situations that can lead to sexual harassment and assault. In these dangerous situations when someone is being threatened and others are present, it is common for people to experience the phenomenon of *diffusion of responsibility* (Darley & Latane, 1968).

A trivial example from my own experience will serve as an example. I taught college classes for more than a quarter of a century, and once every so often I would enter the classroom to find 40–45 students sitting in the dark. Surely everyone must have noticed, but nobody took the initiative to get up and turn on the lights. More than 50 years ago, psychologists Bibb Latane and John Darley demonstrated that in groups of people when help is needed, the responsibility to act seems to get parceled out among the group members. It is much more likely that, if I were meeting with only 3–4 students in the classroom, someone would have turned on the lights. If only one person is present, theoretically they have 100% of the responsibility, but in my classroom of 40, each student has only 2.5%—not enough to spur anyone to action. However, once people understand the phenomenon of diffusion of responsibility, they can recognize this social pressure and take steps to counteract it. Again, it is very difficult to resist a pressure that one cannot name. If we go back to our 3–4 student scenario, it is also more likely in that group that people will talk with one another: "Hey! It's pretty dark in here." "Somebody want to get the lights?" So, communication is also a way to overcome diffusion of responsibility.

Latane and Darley (1970) constructed a model of bystander intervention in which they describe a five-step mental process that people need to go through to act in a situation in which help is needed. First, you must notice the event. Obviously, a person who is totally blind would not know that the lights were off. Second, you need to define it as a problem. Maybe you noticed that the lights were off, but you have a headache and it is actually more comfortable for you if they are off. But if you are trying to read something, it becomes a problem. Third, you must take responsibility for doing something about it. This is perhaps the biggest hurdle—going from "someone ought to do something," to "*I* ought to do something." Fourth, you must decide what you are going to do. In the lights-out scenario, this is not a difficult task although it may be in more complicated situations. Finally, you must act.

If you are an emergency room physician and someone comes in bleeding profusely, you can go through these steps instantaneously because you have been in this situation before and you have extensive training and practice, but what about a situation when you are at a party and there is a drunk person who is getting unwanted sexual attention? You may well be less prepared.

Consider the following scenario: you are on a subway and a man in your car is sexually harassing a woman, who is obviously uncomfortable. There are 30 others in the car. This is such a common occurrence that in some places such as Mexico and Japan, there are cars in which only women and children are permitted to board (Deguchi, 2019; Poska, 2019). The first step toward intervention happens immediately as you notice the intrusive man and the uncomfortable woman, and the second step follows quickly as you see it as a bad situation. That third step, deciding that you should do something, is difficult in such a large group because the responsibility is diffused throughout the bystanders. But you know what diffusion of responsibility is and so you are equipped to overcome it. So, we are on to step four, which is deciding on a course of action. If you have thought about these situations, experienced them before, and perhaps have even practiced your responses, you will be more prepared. For instance, you may call out to the offender in a loud voice, telling him to stop, enlist the cooperation of other bystanders, and/or place yourself between offender and victim.

One of my students described a similar experience. She was walking on campus one evening when a group of obviously drunk men began to yell sexualized and aggressive things at her from a short distance away. She actually feared that they might gang-rape her. But fortunately, as she passed the library, a male student was coming out and saw what was happening. Thinking quickly, he began to pretend that he knew her, began walking with her, and effectively created a social and physical barrier between her and these other men.

When someone is being verbally disrespectful, for example to a co-worker, sometimes it is difficult to come up with an effective response in the moment, although we think of one the next hour or day. If you do, "put it in your pocket"—commit it to memory because you may be able to use it later. And this is probably the simplest technique: sometimes we are stunned by an offensive comment and have no idea what to say but know that we should say something. In these cases, just ask the person to repeat it. You can pretend you did not hear it and simply say, "I'm sorry. What did you say?" Sometimes, people say things without really thinking about their impact. When you ask them to repeat it, they are forced to make the comment again, but this time in a conscious and intentional way. Often, they are embarrassed to do so, in which case you have caused them to think about how they might have offended someone. But if not, you can either pretend you did not hear it a second time and have them state it again, or you may want to confront the person more directly. You do not need to "get out your flip chart," and give an extended lecture to the person. A few words expressing your disapproval can be very effective. Recall from Chapter 4 the story of a man whose friend called him out for harassing a woman in a restaurant and how remarkably effective one instance of confrontation was in changing his outlook and conduct. He never forgot what he learned from the experience and never again harassed anyone.

People who make disrespectful comments are not intending to be offensive, intrusive, and even at times illegal. They think of themselves as witty and charming and expect others to react with approval, and so they often react to challenges with anger, resistance, and defensiveness. It is uncomfortable for many allies (including me) to be confrontational, but practice can help you learn how to tolerate this discomfort. We wish that people would react with, "You're right; thank you for enlightening me," but that kind of response is rare. It is critical to understand that these kinds of responses are more the rule than the exception and that they are no indication that the challenge is ineffective. So, a challenge is akin to planting a metaphorical seed that you may or may or may not have the opportunity to see grow. And so, most interventions must be made as leaps of faith, and even if they may not have affected the person making the comment, sometimes bystanders may be educated and perhaps even inspired to become better allies themselves. The colleague who was challenged by a friend for his harassment said that the experience helped him to "be aware of how I am capable of doing stupid things and how I affect people," and also emboldened him to "do corrections of that nature myself."

Two more stories: one about an immediate response and one about a long delay: I was on a golf trip that included 40 participants, and so in many of the matches, people who did not know one another found themselves in the same foursome. That was the case for me one day when I met three other men on the first tee. There are several tee markers of various distances from the hole and people choose which ones to play based on how far they can hit the golf ball. I am getting older and have lost a lot of distance over the years, and so I told my playing partners on the first tee that I would be hitting from one of the forward markers. One of the men responded with an anti-feminine comment: "Okay, Chris, but understand that we're going to call you a pussy the rest of the round." I had a response "in my pocket." I said, "Well, I don't know; I think [women's golf great] Lorena Ochoa can hit it farther than any of us." To his credit, the young man recognized that he had been offensive and said, "You know what, Chris? We're off to a bad start. I'm sorry." He was clearly not a bad guy and I helped him to understand that he did not win my approval by making a comment disrespectful to women. Again, men make these comments to win the approval of other men, so it will stop when they lose rather than gain social status for their behavior.

And the story about the delayed response: many years ago, I brought the White Ribbon Campaign to my campus. This is a social activism effort to get men involved in working to end men's violence against women. We held awareness events and raised money for our local domestic violence and rape crisis agencies and wore a white ribbon as a pledge never to commit, condone, or remain silent about the all-too-frequent problem of men's violence toward women.

In response, the editor of our campus newspaper wrote a column in which he ridiculed the effort, saying sarcastically, "Oh—I don't know what color ribbon to wear this week," and "You guys aren't making a difference; you're only trying to get in good with women so they'll sleep with you." (He clearly ignored that our fundraising efforts were making a very tangible difference.) In response, I wrote a letter to the paper to criticize the editorial and debate its assumptions. The editor responded with yet another column stating a similar point of view as his first, and I wrote another letter.

At the time, I thought that our conflict was, as my favorite college philosophy professor Tom Mappes was fond of saying, "more heat than light." I did not think that I had convinced him of anything and only took comfort in believing that I may have influenced some readers. So, I was very surprised when, about six years later, I got an email from this editor, apologizing for being disrespectful and explaining that he had learned why this issue was so important. The "seed" took a long time to grow, but grow it did.

In closing, I make several suggestions about vehicles for individual and social change as the cultural conception of masculinity continues to evolve. The first is to examine your own experience. Where and from whom did I learn how people were supposed to be different because of the bodies they inhabit? What assumptions undergirded these lessons? When I reflect on these teachings, what did I decide were distorted, exaggerated, or just plain wrong, and how did I come to these conclusions? I have some stories of masculine personal mythologies sold to boys and how these poor lessons had detrimental effects.

As I reflect on my own boyhood, one of the most painful experiences was occasionally being hit by my father when I misbehaved. Worse than the physical pain was the shame I experienced around having disappointed this man whom I loved so deeply. I do not recall his doing this to any of my three sisters; I think he assumed that boys should be able to "take it," and he believed that physical punishment was beneficial to us. Thus, he justified this violence by thinking it was an act of love. I had a brother who was a year and a half younger than me and since we often got into trouble together, we usually were punished together. We always cried during these beatings but once my brother refused to cry and instead glared at my father with anger. My father then told me that I should be more like my brother, that boys should never cry. It was perhaps his worst moment I experienced with him as my parent.

Children are the only people who can legally be hit in the United States, not only by parents but in many states, by school authorities. Although police and correctional officers can use force to subdue a resistant person, they are supposed to use it minimally and as a last resort. I have often seen posts on social media from those who think that the problem with "kids nowadays" is that they suffer from a lack of respect and self-discipline because so many parents do not hit them. They express pride in their own childhood suffering, writing things like "Now I suffer from a condition. It's called respect." I think that they have confused deference for respect. I very much respected my father, but not for hitting me. He did many great things as a parent and thankfully the beatings were not very frequent. More than 80% of United States parents physically punish their children (Gershoff & Grogan-Kaylor, 2016).

What does the research tell us about the effects of physical punishment on children? It is apparent that mild and occasional physical punishment does not have long-term negative effects, but the more often and more severely a parent deploys it, and the less that it is counterbalanced with positive interactions between parent and child, the more the child is at risk for a wide variety of poor outcomes in adulthood, including depression, anxiety, substance abuse, aggression, and criminality (Smith, 2012; Vendantam, 2002). In fact, the effects of physical punishment are similar to those of physical abuse across cultures (Gershoff et al., 2018). Most psychologists who know of this research recommend that parents use physical punishment mildly and rarely, if at all, and that if they decide to use it, it should be accompanied by an explanation of the incorrect behavior as well as an opportunity to learn the correct one and be reinforced for it.

A single incident of physical punishment is unlikely to cause lasting ill effects any more than eating one unhealthy meal, smoking a single cigarette, or watching one violent movie. The effects are subtle, cumulative, and sometimes indirect. The more frequently and intensely we have these experiences, the more likely we are to suffer from them as they add up.

Sometimes masculine myths are idiosyncratic to families and passed down from father to son. Like broader cultural gender myths, they can sometimes prevent the son from accessing useful resources with which to live his life if he fails to think critically about these distorted lessons. These teachings have the potential to be even more powerful since they are learned in the context of a father–son bond. I will relate two stories of family myth transmission, one from a psychotherapy client and the other from an audience member at one of my presentations.

The client was a male college student I saw for a few sessions at a college counseling center. He exhibited very little emotion—a blunted appearance. He had very few interests except for sports. Like many boys, his dream was to someday be a great athlete, but also like most boys, he lacked the physical talents to realize this ambition. Still, he played in almost every sport he could. I asked him to tell me about his relationship with his father, whereupon it was clear that his father was also highly invested in his son being a good athlete. He explained, "My father came to every game. Afterwards, we would sit down together and he would tell me what I had done wrong and how I could improve." I asked if they ever discussed what he had done well. His answer: "Never."

It soon became apparent to me that this young man believed, without knowing it consciously, that being a good athlete was the only way to win his father's love. But every time he tried, his father responded with a detailed list of his son's inadequacies, telling the son that he was unlovable without saying so directly. My diagnosis for this young man was dysthymia, a chronic, personality-based depression. He was a melancholy, "glass half-empty" kind of person. Even if he experienced occasional pleasure it only served as a reminder of the pain that was to come. Dysthymia, like most chronic conditions, usually requires long-term treatment, as in general, the longer one has experienced the mental health problem, the more difficult it is to recover from it. And, when a dysthymic person experiences significantly negative events (for instance, if a loved one should die or he were to lose his job), they are prone to developing major depression, which, in combination with the dysthymia, is sometimes called "double depression."

There was no time to do extensive treatment with this young man, as the end of the academic year was at hand and he was going back to his hometown at that point. The best I could do would be to make some inroads into some of his assumptions about the world and about his father. He was playing in an ice hockey game between two of our sessions and so, as homework, I asked him to sit down afterwards and make a list of the things that he had done *well* during the game. He immediately asked, "Can I also write down what I did wrong?" My response:

"No. You're already really good at that. We're trying to learn something new here." He was clearly uncomfortable with the exercise, which he seemed to view as a sort of betrayal of his father. Still he completed it and seemed to get a little relief from it, but there was such a long way for him to go if he were ever to become mentally healthy.

Same theme, this time with an audience member: A few years ago, I was giving a presentation and in the course of my talk I summarized this research and criticized the wisdom of physically punishing children. A young man in the audience became visibly upset during this part of the presentation and came up to me to talk after it was over. The source of his malaise was, as one might guess, that his father punished him physically and that he loved his father. He seemed to believe that love meant that, as a son, he could never be critical of his father's actions—that if he were, it would mean that he did not love his father.

The big problem with this attitude of foreclosure is that if a parent is seen as infallible, the child will try to emulate the parent if they should have children of their own and thus repeat the same mistakes. I have heard many people, especially men, make statements such as, "Yeah, my daddy used to beat me good and it was the best thing he ever did for me because I was a knucklehead and couldn't learn any other way." As a psychologist, it is always fascinating to me that these people exhibit more identification with the aggressor in these events than with the victim, despite the fact that they *were* the victim!–a real testament to the larger-than-life presence of fathers in many sons' lives. It is clear that those who romanticize their own trauma are highly likely to pass it on, perpetuating an intergenerational transmission of violence.

My words of wisdom for men, especially young ones: your father, although he likely did the best he could with the resources available to him at the time and likely loved you deeply, was not infallible. You can believe that he made some mistakes, forgive him for those errors, and still love him at the same time. If you are able to see him as a sometimes-flawed human being, you can resolve to build on the positive things you learned from him and avoid making some of the same mistakes. If you do not, you are likely to repeat his errors and cause needless damage. So—think of yourself as "Dad 2.0."

Now we come to the end of our journey into the world of cultural masculinity. I hope that reading this book has helped you to become more aware of the gendered demands that are made on you from so many forces, and will undertake the process of thinking critically about these demands and resisting them when they are not in concert with your goals and values, and that you will help others do so as well.

# REFERENCES

Acker, S. E. (2013). *Unclenching our fists: Abusive men on the journey to nonviolence.* Nashville, TN: Vanderbilt University Press.

Addis, M. E., & Hoffman, E. (2020). *The psychology of men in context.* New York: Routledge.

Addis, M. E., & Mahalik, J. R. (2003). Men, masculinity, and the contexts of help seeking. *American Psychologist, 58,* 5–14.

Alexander, M. (2012). *The new Jim Crow: Mass incarceration in the age of colorblindness.* New York: The New Press.

American Sociological Association (2015). Women more likely than men to initiate divorces, but not non-marital break-ups. Retrieved May 5, 2020 from https://www.asanet.org/press-center/press-releases/women-more-likely-men-initiate-divorces-not-non-marital-breakups.

Anderson, K. J., Kanner, M., & Elsayegh, N. (2009). Are feminists man haters? Feminists' and nonfeminists' attitudes toward men. *Psychology of Women Quarterly, 33,* 216–224.

Angier, N. (1999). *Woman: An intimate geography.* Boston: Houghton-Mifflin.

Aronson, E. (2001). *How the Columbine massacre could have been avoided.* Paper presented at the Annual Convention of the American Psychological Association, San Francisco, CA.

Aronson, E. (2008). *The social animal* (10th ed.). New York: Worth.

Asch, S. E. (1965). Effects of group pressure upon the modification and distortion of judgments. In H. Proshansky & B. Seidenberg (Eds.), *Basic studies in social psychology.* New York: Holt, Rinehart, and Winston.

Austrian boy overjoyed with new shoes (1940/2020). Retrieved January, 9, 2020 from https://www.google.com/search?q=image+of+world+war+II+boy+overjoyed+with+new+shoes&sxsrf=ACYBGNRHqDsTJdAXuc0uBv3rk6Oj8cThfw:1580314877833&tbm=isch&source=iu&ictx=1&fir=U0Yuau38zYRcVM%253A%252Ce8LY1Hm0MZLqMM%252C_&vet=1&usg=AI4_-kR6eN9-1JOSPrsljFBASvEEAklXww&sa=X&ved=2ahUKEwiGuLTXm6nnAhVNl3IEHfl_AxoQ9QEwAHoECAYQBQ#imgrc=U0Yuau38zYRcVM.

Baron, R. A., & Branscome, N. R. (2011). *Social psychology* (13th ed.). Boston: Pearson.

Bartholomew, B. D., Dill, K. E., Anderson, K. B., & Lindsay, J. J. (2003). The proliferation of media violence and its economic underpinnings. In D. A. Gentile (Ed.), *Media violence and children: A complete guide for parents and professionals.* Westport, CT: Praeger.

Basow, S. (1992). *Gender: Stereotypes and roles* (3rd ed.). Monterey, CA: Brooks/Cole.
Bem, S. L. (1993). *The lenses of gender: Transforming the debate on sexual inequality.* New Haven, CT: Yale University Press.
Bem, S. L. (1998). *An unconventional family.* New Haven, CT: Yale University Press.
Berkowitz, A. D. (2004). Feature article: Emerging challenges and issues for the social norms approach. *The Report on Social Norms, 3*(7), 1, 7.
Berkowitz, A. D. (2014). Personal communication.
Blake, M. (2015). Mad men: inside the men's rights movement—and the army of misogynists it trolls and spawned. Originally published in *Mother Jones*; retrieved January 30, 2020 from https://www.motherjones.com/politics/2015/01/warren-farrell-mens-rights-movement-feminism-misogyny-trolls/.
Campbell, R. (2012). The neurobiology of sexual assault: Implications for law enforcement, prosecution, and victim advocacy. Retrieved March 3, 2020 from https://nij.ojp.gov/media/video/24056.
Carr, E., Li Puma, K., Wheeler, K. A., Yuditsky, T. J., Frankel, L., & Kilmartin, C. T. (2002). *Sexism, masculinity, and attitudes towards sexual assault in college men: A social norms intervention.* Paper presented at the Spring Convention of the Virginia Psychological Association.
Cohn, A., & Zeichner, A. (2006). Effects of masculine identity and gender role stress on aggression in men. *Psychology of Men & Masculinity, 7*(4), 179–190.
Coltrane, S. (1998). Theorizing masculinities in contemporary social science. In D. L. Anselmi & A. L. Law (Eds.), *Questions of gender: perspectives and paradoxes* (pp. 76–88). Boston: McGraw-Hill.
Coontz, S. (2016). *The way we never were: American families and the nostalgia trap.* New York: Basic Books.
Coontz, S. (1997). *The way we really are: Coming to terms with America's changing families.* New York: Basic Books.
Courtenay, W. H. (2011). *Dying to be men: Psychosocial, environmental, and biobehavioral directions in promoting the health of men and boys.* New York: Routledge.
Crosby, A. E., Ortega, L., & Stevens, M. R. (2013). Suicides—United States, 2005–2009. *Mortality and Morbidity Weekly Review, 62* Supplement, 179–183.
Darley, J. M., & Latane, B. (1968). Bystander intervention in emergencies: Diffusion of responsibility. *Journal of Personality and Social Psychology, 8,* 377–383.
de Becker, G. (1997). *The gift of fear, and other survival signals that protect us from violence.* New York: Random House.
Deguchi, M. (2019). Personal communication.
de Waal, F. B. M. (2005). *Our inner ape: What primate behavior tells us about human nature.* Paper presented at the Annual Convention of the American Psychological Association, Washington, DC.
Dines, G. (2013). *Hypersexualized media as a public health threat.* In Interdisciplinary meetings on developing a social-ecological response to hypersexualized media as a public health threat, Richmond, VA (J. A. Johnston, Chair).
Dutton, D. G. (2011). *Rethinking domestic violence.* Vancouver, BC: UBC Press.
Dutton, D. G., & Golant, S. K. (1995). *The batterer: A psychological profile.* New York: Basic Books.
Eagly, A. H., Nater, C., Miller, D. I., Kaufmann, M., & Sczesny, S. (2019). Gender stereotypes have changed: A cross-temporal meta-analysis of U.S. public opinion polls from 1946 to 2018. *American Psychologist, 75,* 301–315.
Ehrenreich, B. (1983). *The hearts of men: American dreams and the flight from commitment.* Garden City, NY: Anchor.

Ehrmann, J. (with P. Ehrmann and G. Jordan) (2011). *InsideOut Coaching: How sports can transform lives.* New York: Simon and Schuster.
Eliot, L. (2009). *Pink brain, blue brain: How small differences grow into troublesome gaps—and what we can do about it.* Boston: Houghton Mifflin Harcourt.
Englar-Carlson, M., & Kiselica, M. S. (2013). Affirming the strengths in men: A positive masculinity approach to assisting male clients. *Journal of Counseling and Development,* 91, 399–409.
Episode 16: Preventing sexual harassment in academia (2020). Retrieved February 28, 2020 from https://podcasts.apple.com/us/podcast/dotedu/id1470285055?i=1000466529751&fbclid=IwAR11YD3g-_bVqMl8z41kXfqqJuz1RgjKlXTVxwJP7bp63jmtrufZjnB17IE.
Fagen, J. L., & Anderson, P. B. (2012). Constructing masculinity in response to women's sexual advances. *Archives of Sexual Behavior,* 41, 261–270.
Farrell, B. S. (2015). *Actions needed to address sexual assaults of male service members.* Washington, D.C.: United States Government Accountability Office.
Farrell, W. (1991). Men as success objects. *Utne Reader,* May/June, 81–84.
Fazio, R. H., & Olson, M. A. (2003). Implicit measures in social cognition research: Their meaning and use. *Annual Review of Psychology,* 54, 297–327.
Federal Bureau of Investigation. (2016). FBI Releases 2015 Crime Statistics from the National Incident-Based Reporting System, Encourages Transition. Retrieved from Washington DC: https://ucr.fbi.gov/nibrs/2015/resource-pages/nibrs-2015_summary_final-1.pdf.
Fine, C. (2017). *Testosterone Rex: Unmaking the myths of our gendered minds.* New York: Norton.
Foubert, J. D., Clark-Taylor, A., & Wall, A. F. (2019). Is campus rape primarily a serial or one-time problem? Evidence from a multicampus study. *Violence Against Women,* 26, 296–311.
Francis, R. C. (2004). *Why men won't ask for directions: The seductions of sociobiology.* Princeton, NJ: Princeton University Press.
Gentile, D. A. (Ed.) (2003). *Media violence and children: A complete guide for parents and professionals.* Westport, CT: Praeger.
Gershoff, E. T., & Grogan-Kaylor, A. (2016). Spanking and child outcomes: Old controversies and new meta-analyses. *Journal of Family Psychology,* 30, 453–469.
Gershoff, E. T., Goodman, G. S., Miller-Perin, C. L., Holden, G. W., Jackson, Y., & Kazdin, A. E. (2018). The strength of the causal evidence against physical punishment of children and its implications for parents, psychologists, and policymakers. *American Psychologist,* 73, 626–638.
Glick, P. (2005). *Ambivalent gender ideologies and perceptions of the legitimacy and stability of gender hierarchy.* Paper presented in symposium: "New wave sexism research: Tangled webs of feminism, romance, and inequality" (S. T. Fiske, Chair). Annual Convention of the American Psychological Association, Washington, DC.
Glick, P., & Fiske, S. T. (2001). An ambivalent alliance: Hostile and benevolent sexism as complementary justifications for gender inequality. *American Psychologist,* 56(2), 109–118.
Goldenberg, S. (2005). Why women are poor at science, by Harvard president. Retrieved April 23, 2020 from https://www.theguardian.com/science/2005/jan/18/educationsgendergap.genderissues.
Gottman, J. M., & Silver, N. (1999). *The seven principles for making marriage work.* New York: Crown.
Grossman, J. S. (2017, December 4). Vice President Pence's "never dine alone with a woman" rule isn't honorable. It's probably illegal. Retrieved April 30, 2020 from https://www.vox.com/the-big-idea/2017/3/31/15132730/pence-women-alone-rule-graham-discrimination.

*The Guardian* (2009). Polanski was not guilty of "rape-rape" says Whoopi Goldberg. Retrieved February 28, 2020 from https://www.theguardian.com/film/2009/sep/29/roman-polanski-whoopi-goldberg.

Halpern, D. F., Eliot, L., Bigler, R. S., Fabes, R. A., Hanish, L. D., Hyde, J., Liben, L. S., & Martin, C. L. (2011). The pseudoscience of single-sex schooling. *Science*, 333, 1706–1707.

Hammer, J. H., & Good, G.E. (2010). Positive psychology: An empirical examination of beneficial aspects of endorsement of masculine norms. *Psychology of Men and Masculinity*, 11, 303–318.

Harvey, S. (2014). *Act like a lady, think like a man: What men really think about love, relationships, intimacy, and commitment.* New York: HarperCollins.

Hax, C. (2009, March 8). *Carolyn Hax* (advice column). *Washington Post*, C7.

Huizinga, D., Weiher, A. W., Espiritu, R., & Esbensen, F. (2003). Delinquency and crime: Some highlights from the Denver Youth Survey. In T. P. Thornberry & M. D. Krohn (Eds.), *Taking stock of delinquency: An overview of findings from contemporary longitudinal studies.* New York: Kluwer Academic/Plenum.

Hyde, J. S. (2005). The gender similarities hypothesis. *American Psychologist*, 60, 581–592.

"I have a family to feed." (2020). Retrieved January 29, 2020 from https://www.google.com/search?tbm=isch&sxsrf=ACYBGNTkM1FSw4kEp2YwG-xE-jn7inKsg%3A1580315066143&sa=1&ei=urExXsaoCLK0ytMP9Y2U6AM&q=latrell+sprewell+i+got+a+family+to+feed&oq=latrell+sprewell+I+&gs_l=img.1.0.0i24l2.910.4582..6962...5.0..0.638.2335.5j1j1j1j0j2......0....1..gws-wiz-img.......0i67j0j35i39.a-grI0j_ijo#imgrc=FVK3YX4WxywaCM.

Infurna, F. J., Gerstorf, D., & Lachman, M. E. (2020). Midlife in the 2020s: Opportunity and challenges. *American Psychologist*, 75, 470–485.

Jacques-Tiura, A. J., Abbey, A., Wegner, R., Pierce, J., Pegram, S. E., & Woerner, J. (2015). Friends matter: Protective and harmful aspects of male friendships associated with past-year sexual aggression in a community sample of young men. *American Journal of Public Health*, 105, 1001–1007.

Jaques, E. (1965). Death and the mid-life crisis. *International Journal of Psychoanalysis*, 46, 502–514.

Johnson, A. J. (Ed.) (2015). *Religion and men's violence against women.* New York: Springer.

Jung, C. G. (1959/1989). Concerning the archetypes: With special reference to the anima concept. In C. G. Jung, R. F. C. Hull (Translator), & J. Beebe (Ed.), *Aspects of the masculine* (pp. 115–122). Princeton, NJ: Princeton University Press.

Katz, J. (2014). Personal communication.

Kawakami, K., Dovidio, J. F., Moll, J., Hermsen, S., & Russin, A. (2000). Just say no (to stereotyping): Effects of training in the negation of stereotypic associations on stereotype activation. *Journal of Personality and Social Psychology*, 78(5), 871–888.

Keen, S. (1991). *Fire in the belly: On being a man.* New York: Bantam.

Kerman, P. (2011). *Orange is the new black: My year in a women's prison.* New York: Random House.

Kilmartin, C. T. (2014). Counseling men to prevent sexual violence. In M. Englar-Carlson, M. Evans, & T. Duffey (Eds.), *A counselor's guide to working with men.* Alexandria, VA: American Counseling Association.

Kilmartin, C. T. (2017). Men as allies. In J. Schwarz (Ed.), *Counseling women across the lifespan: Empowerment, advocacy, and intervention.* New York: Springer.

Kilmartin, C. T. (2020). *Crimes against nature.* Video. Retrieved April 16, 2020 from https://vimeo.com/139330024.

Kilmartin, C., & Allison, J. (2007). *Men's violence against women: Theory, research, and activism.* Mahwah, NJ: Erlbaum.

Kilmartin, C. T., & Berkowitz, A. D. (2005). *Sexual assault in context: Teaching college men about gender*. Mahwah, NJ: Erlbaum.

Kilmartin, C. T., Semelsberger, R., Dye, S.Boggs, E., & Kolar, D. W. (2015). A behavior intervention to reduce sexism in college men. *Gender Issues*, 32, 97–110.

Kilmartin, C. T., & Smiler, A. P. (2015). *The masculine self* (5th ed.). Cornwall-on-Hudson, NY: Sloan.

Kilmartin, C., Smith, T., Green, A., Kuchler, M., Heinzen, H., & Kolar, D. (2008). A real time social norms intervention to reduce male sexism. *Sex Roles: A Journal of Research*, 59, 264–273.

Kimmel, M. S. (2006). *Manhood in America: A cultural history* (2nd ed.). New York: Oxford University Press.

Kimmel, M. (2008). *Guyland: The perilous world where boys become men*. New York: Harper.

Kirwan Institute (2020). Understanding implicit bias. Retrieved March 12, 2020 from http://kirwaninstitute.osu.edu/researchandstrategicinitiatives/#opportunitycommunities.

Kivel, P. (1992). *Men's work: How to stop the violence that tears our lives apart*. Center City, MN: Hazleden.

Koss, M. P., Gidycz, C. A., & Wisniewski, N. (1987). The scope of rape: Incidence and prevalence of sexual aggression and victimization in a national sample of higher education students. *Journal of Consulting and Clinical Psychology*, 55, 162–170.

Kramarae, C., & Treichler, P. (1986). "Feminism is the radical notion that women are people." Retrieved April 11, 2019 from www.beverlymcphail.com/feminismradicalnotion.html.

Latane, B., & Darley, J. M. (1970). *The unresponsive bystander: Why doesn't he help?* New York: Appleton-Century-Crofts.

Lawrence, A. (2020). *Staying in the game: The playbook for beating workplace sexual harassment*. New York: Tarcher Peregree.

Lerner, G. (1986). *The creation of patriarchy*. New York: Oxford University Press.

Levant, R. F., Hall, R. J., Williams, C. M., & Hasan, N. T. (2009). Gender differences in alexithymia. *Psychology of Men & Masculinity*, 10(3), 190–203.

Levant, R. F., & Pryor, S. (2020). *The tough standard: The hard truths about masculinity and violence*. New York: Oxford University Press.

Levinson, D. J., Darrow, C. N., Klein, E. B., Levinson, M. H., & McKee, B. (1978). *The seasons of a man's life*. New York: Random House.

Lisak, D. (1991). Sexual aggression, masculinity, and fathers. *Signs*, 16, 238–262.

Lisak, D. (1997). Male gender socialization and the perpetration of sexual abuse. In R. F. Levant, & G. R. Brooks (Eds.), *Men and sex* (pp. 156–177). New York: Wiley.

Lisak, D., & Miller, P. M. (2002). Repeat rape and multiple offending among undetected rapists. *Violence and Victims*, 17(1), 73–84.

Livingston, D. W. (2011). What can tolerance teach us about prejudice? Profile of the nonprejudiced. In L. R. Troop & R. K. Mallett (Eds.), *Moving beyond prejudice: Pathways to positive intergroup relations*. Washington, DC: American Psychological Association.

Long, D. (1987). Working with men who batter. In M. Scher, M. Stevens, G. Good, & G. A. Eichenfield (Eds.), *Handbook of counseling and psychotherapy with men*. Newbury Park, CA: Sage.

Lynch, J. R., & Kilmartin, C. (2013). *Overcoming masculine depression: The pain behind the mask* (2nd ed.). New York: Routledge.

Markus, J. (2020). The dudes who won't wear masks: Face coverings are a powerful tool, but health authorities can't simply ignore the reasons that some people refuse to use them. Retrieved June 24, 2020 from https://www.theatlantic.com/ideas/archive/2020/06/dudes-who-wont-wear-masks/613375/.

McCambridge, R. (2019). In Georgia, women may receive a death sentence for choosing abortion. *Non-profit Quarterly*, retrieved April 30, 2020 from https://nonprofitquarterly.org/in-georgia-women-may-receive-a-death-sentence-for-choosing-abortion/.

McIntosh, P. (1988). White privilege and male privilege: A personal account of coming to see correspondences through work in women's studies. Working paper No. 189. Wellesley, MA: Wellesley Center for Research on Women.

McIntosh, P. (2009). White privilege: Unpacking the invisible knapsack. In V. Taylor, N. Whittier, & L. J. Rupp (Eds.), *Feminist frontiers* (8th ed.) (pp. 120–126). Boston: McGraw-Hill.

Meyerson, D., & Tompkins, M. (2007). Tempered radicals as institutional change agents: The case of advancing gender equity at the University of Michigan. *Harvard Journal of Law and Gender*, 30, 303–322.

Molla, M. T. (2013). Expected years of life free of chronic condition–induced activity limitations—United States, 1999–2008. *Mortality and Morbidity Weekly Review*, 62 Supplement, 86–92.

Munch, A. (2013). Personal communication.

Nelson, J. B. (1997). *Male sexuality, masculine spirituality*. Paper presented at the 22nd Conference on Men and Masculinity, Collegeville, MN.

*The New Yorker* (2018). After the Kavanaugh allegations, Republicans offer a shocking defense: Sexual assault isn't a big deal. Retrieved February 28, 2020 from https://www.newyorker.com/news/our-columnists/after-the-kavanaugh-allegations-republicans-offer-a-shocking-defense-sexual-assault-isnt-a-big-deal.

Peter, J., & Valkenburg, P. M. (2007). Adolescents' exposure to a sexualized media environment and their notions of women as sex objects. *Sex Roles*, 56, 381–395.

Plank, L. (2019, September 15). How the patriarchy is killing men—and how feminism might save them. *Washington Post*, B3.

Plank, L. (2019a). *For the love of men: A new vision for mindful masculinity*. New York: St. Martin's Press.

Pleck, J. H. (1994). *Men's studies institute award presentation speech*. Paper presented at the 19th National Conference on Men and Masculinity, Providence, Rhode Island.

Poska, A. (2019). Personal communication.

Quinn-Nilas, C., Goncalves, M. K., Kennett, D. J., & Grant, A. (2018). A thematic analysis of men's sexual compliance with unwanted, non-coercive sex. *Psychology of Men and Masculinity*, 19, 203–211.

Raver, J. L., & Gelfand, M. J. (2005). Beyond the individual victim: Linking sexual harassment, team processes, and team performance. *Academy of Management Journal*, 48, 387–400.

Ridley, M. (2017). Robot farming will bring great benefits to all. *The Rational Optimist*. Retrieved January 23, 2020 from www.rationaloptimist.com/blog/robot-farm-machinery/.

Rosenkoetter, L. I., Rosenkoetter, S. E., Osretich, R. A., & Acock, A. C. (2004). Mitigating the harmful effects of violent television. *Journal of Applied Developmental Psychology*, 25, 25–47.

Rosin, H. (2012). *The end of men (and the rise of women)*. New York: Penguin.

Rudman, L. A., & Fairchild, K. (2007). The F word: Is feminism incompatible with beauty and romance? *Psychology of Women Quarterly*, 31, 125–136.

Rudman, L. A., & Glick, P. (2008). *The social psychology of gender: How power and intimacy shape gender relations*. New York: Guilford.

Rudman, L. A., & Phelan, J. E. (2007). The interpersonal power of feminism: Is feminism good for relationships? *Sex Roles*, 57, 787–799.

Sadler, A. G., Booth, B. M., Cook, B. L., & Doebbeling, B. N. (2003). Factors associated with women's risk of rape in the military environment. *American Journal of Industrial Medicine*, 43, 262–273.

Sanday, P. R. (1981). The socio-cultural context of rape: A cross-cultural study. *Journal of Social Issues*, 37, 5–27.

Sanday, P. R. (1996). *A woman scorned: Acquaintance rape on trial*. New York: Doubleday.

Sanday, P. R. (2007). *Fraternity gang rape: Sex, brotherhood, and privilege on campus*. New York: New York University Press.

Sapolsky, R. M. (1997). The trouble with testosterone: Will boys just be boys? In R. M. Sapolsky, *The trouble with testosterone, and other essays on the biology of the human predicament* (pp. 147–159). New York: Touchstone.

Sapr.mil (2020). United States Department of Defense, *Sexual assault prevention and response*. Retrieved March 3, 2020 from https://www.sapr.mil/reports.

Sax, L. (2017). *Why gender matters: What parents and teachers need to know about the emerging science of sex differences*. New York: Crown.

Schwartz, J. P., McDermott, R. C., & Martino-Harms, J. W. (2016). Men's sexism: Causes, correlates, and trends in research. In Y. J. Wong, S. R. Wester, Y. J. Wong, & S. R. Wester (Eds.), *APA handbook of men and masculinities*. (pp. 483–501). Washington, DC: American Psychological Association.

The Sentencing Project (2013). Gender differences in incarceration rates. Retrieved from Washington, DC: www.sentencingproject.org/wp-content/uploads/2016/06/The-Color-of-Justice-Racial-and-Ethnic-Disparity-in-State-Prisons.pdf.

Sheehy, G. (1976). *Passages*. New York: Dutton.

Sifneos, P. E. (1972). *Short-term psychotherapy and emotional crisis*. Cambridge, MA: Harvard University Press.

Smiler, A. P., & Kilmartin, C. T. (2019). *The masculine self* (6th ed.). Cornwall-on-Hudson, NY: Sloan.

Smith, B. L. (2012). The case against spanking: Physical discipline is slowly declining as some studies reveal lasting harms for children. *Monitor on Psychology*, 43(4), 60–63.

Stern, G. (2010). Personal communication in the context of US Naval Academy sexual harassment and assault prevention education (SHAPE) training.

Stice, E., Marti, N., Spoor, S., Presnell, K., & Shaw, H. (2008). Dissonance and healthy weight eating disorder prevention programs: Long-term effects from a randomized efficacy trial. *Journal of Consulting and Clinical Psychology*, 76, 329–340.

Tavris, C. (1992). *The mismeasure of woman*. New York: Simon and Schuster.

Tavris, C., & Aronson, E. (2008). *Mistakes were made, but not by me: Why we justify foolish beliefs, bad decisions, and hurtful acts*. New York: Houghton Mifflin Harcourt.

Tennyson, A. (1847/1891). *The complete works of Alfred, Lord Tennyson*. New York: Frederick A. Stokes.

Thornhill, R., & Palmer, C. T. (2000). *A natural history of rape: Biological bases of sexual coercion*. Cambridge, MA: MIT Press.

Vendantam, S. (2002, June 26). Study: Harm outweighs benefits of spanking. *The Washington Post*, A3.

A Voice for Men (2014). Soften the fuck up! Retrieved April 21, 2020 from https://avoiceformen.com/featured/soften-the-fuck-up/.

Vox.com (2019). Our incel problem: How a support group for the dateless became one of the internet's most dangerous subcultures. Retrieved March 3, 2020 from https://www.vox.com/the-highlight/2019/4/16/18287446/incel-definition-reddit.

Wilkins, C. L., Wellman, J. D., Flavin, E. L., & Manrique, J. A. (2018). When men perceive anti-male bias: Status-legitimizing beliefs increase discrimination against women. *Psychology of Men and Masculinity*, 19, 282–290.

Williams, J. E., Nieto, J., Sanford, C. P., Couper, D. J., & Tyroler, H. A. (2002). The association between trait anger and incident stroke risk: The atherosclerosis risk in communities (ARIC) study. *Stroke*, 33(13), 13–20.

Willness, C. R., Steel, P., & Lee, K. (2007). A meta-analysis of the antecedents and consequences of workplace sexual harassment. *Personnel Psychology*, 60, 127–162.

Wong, Y. J., Klann, E. M., Bijelic, N., & Aguayo, F. (2017). The link between men's zero-sum gender beliefs and mental health: Findings from Chile and Croatia. *Psychology of Men and Masculinity*, 18, 12–19.

Yourdictionary.com (2020). Definition of abstraction. Retrieved February 22, 2020 from https://www.yourdictionary.com/abstraction.

Youtube.com (2019). *Here is a man who understands women*. Retrieved December 21, 2019 from https://www.youtube.com/watch?v=oh-MEevD7zI.

Youtube.com (2020). *Life of privilege explained in a $100 race*. Retrieved January 30, 2020 from https://www.youtube.com/watch?v=4K5fbQ1-zps.

Zell, E., Krizen, Z., & Teeter, S. R. (2015). Evaluating gender similarities and differences using metasynthesis. *American Psychologist*, 70, 10–20.

# INDEX

*Act Like a Lady; Think Like a Man* 15
Addis, M. 3, 15
adversarial sexual beliefs 83, 120
advertising 61–65
alexithymia 112
alcohol 53, 57, 59, 61–64, 72, 80, 84, 99, 105–07
allies with women, male 20, 80, 84, 117–19
alpha male 38, 45
Angier, N. 42
antifemininity x, 19–20, 78, 99, 120, 123
*antisocial personality disorder* 38–39, 77, 84
Aronson, E. 86, 94, 119
Asch, S. 56–57
athletics ix, 1, 3, 5, 11–12, 16, 20, 29–31, 60, 78, 99, 111, 113, 116, 125

*Back to the Future* 45
Batali, M. 72
"battle of the sexes," xi, 40
Becker, R. 14–15, 17, 20, 25, 47, 65
Beer 1, 45, 52–53, 59, 61–65, 100, 113
*belief in a just world* 7
Bem, S. 13, 20, 104, 109–110
benevolent sexism 74,102–104
Berkowitz, A. 10
Black Lives Matter 75–76
Borg, B. 29
Bryant, K. 5
bystander intervention 84, 93, 95, 121

Campbell, R. 81–82, 90
Chamberlain, W. 42
child custody 8
chivalry (benevolent sexism) 74, 102–104
Cho, S. 97
chromosomes 21, 37, 46–47
Clinton, H. 119
Coltrane, S. 44
*confirmation bias* 17, 26, 30
conformity 3. 52, 56–57, 65–66, 98–100, 111
Coolidge, C. 40
Coolidge effect, 40
Coolidge, G. 40
Coontz, S. 69
corporal punishment 124–25
Cosby, B. 72, 84
Covid-19 pandemic 116
*Creation of Patriarchy, The* 67, 81
*Crimes Against Nature* xii, 111
Crystal, B. 32

Darley, J. 121
Darwin, C. 23, 39
*Defending the Caveman* 14, 25
deWaal, F. 45
*differential reproductive investment* 40–42
*diffusion of responsibility* 121–22
Dines, G. 51, 64–65
divorce 8, 12, 16, 34, 113, 116
Dworkin, A. 6

Eagly, A.
*Eat What You Want and Die Like a Man* 61
Ehrenreich, B. 47
Ehrmann, J. 83
Eliot, L. 20, 36, 110
emotion x, 1, 13, 18, 20, 35, 52, 61, 63, 69–71, 78, 83, 90, 112
*End of Men, The* 97
enlightened self-interest approach to prevention 87, 89–90, 118
Evolutionary Psychology, *see* Sociobiology

*false consensus* 52
Farrell, W. 8
feminism 5–6, 8, 16, 50–51, 90, 97, 102, 116–17
fight, flight, or freeze response 39–40
*file drawer effect* 28
Fine, C. 38, 42
Fiske, S. 102
Floyd, G. 75
Ford, C. 80
Foubert, J. 89
Francis, R. 46–47
fraternities 31–34, 57, 70, 98–99
Freud, S. 47
friendship x, 24, 30, 34, 50–51, 54–55, 59–60, 65, 85, 98–99, 112, 122–23
*fundamental attribution error* 28–30

Gardner, R. 48
gender; definition 1–4; historical division of labor 67–73, 96; schema 26–28, 104, 109–110; situational pressure 2–3, 10, 26, 29, 42, 60, 121; socialization 1, 78
Glick, P. 101–03
Goldberg, W. 80
Golding, W. 16
Goldsmith, J. 62
Gray, J. 12–15, 17, 20
*greater status legitimizing belief* 7
*Guyland* 57

Harvey, S. 15–17
Hax, C. 101
health, mental x, 3, 12, 38, 61, 98, 116, 125
health, physical 115–16
Hill, J. 2
Hills, H. 3–4
Hoffman, E. 3
homophobia x, 43–44, 62, 102–103, 117

incarceration 7–8, 10, 39, 68, 84, 91
"Incel" (involuntary celibate) 83
Implicit bias 119–20

Jaques, E. 16
Jung, C. 113

Katz, J. 44
Kavanaugh, B. 29, 80
Kerman, P. 7–8
Kilmartin, C. 5–6
Kimmel, M. 31, 57–58
King, B. 40–41
King, K. 15, 17
Kivel, P. ix
Kosgei, B. 22
Koss, M. 92
*Knitting with Balls* 61
Kramarae, C. 50
Kuchler, M. 55

Latane, B. 121
*Lenses of Gender, The* 28
Lerner, G. 67–68, 70, 81
Lisak, D. 83
*Lord of the Flies* 16
Lynch, J. 25, 48, 78

"male bashing" 15–17, 44, 75, 107, 117
male "midlife crisis" 16
Mappes, T. 123
Martin, T. 75
McIntosh, P. 5
#metoo movement 44, 72
*Men are from Mars; Women are from Venus* 12–14, 24, 34
men's rights movement 8–9
men's rights activists (MRAs), *see* Men's rights movement
men's societies 31, 70
Men's Studies 4
Military, 1, 5, 6, 7
*Mistakes Were Made, but not by Me* 119
mortality gap 4, 115–16

Nadal, R. 12
Nasser, L. 84
Nash, O. 40, 42
*Natural History of Rape, A* 41
Nelson, J. 112
Nyad, D. 48

Ochoa, L. 20, 123
*Orange is the new Black* 8
O'Reilly, B. 72
Ovid 113

Packard, G. 44–45
*Pain Behind the Mask, The* 25

Pak, S. 20
Palmer, C. 41, 44
Pavlov, I. 39
Pence, M. 72–74
Peterson, J. 37
*Pink Brain, Blue Brain* 37
Plank, L. 3, 97
Pleck, J. 40
*pluralistic ignorance* 52
Polanski, R. 80
pornography 41, 51, 64–65, 113
*Power of the Pussy, The* 15
prejudice 7–8, 13, 18, 21, 61, 65, 95–96, 103; reduction of 94, 96, 119–20
prison, *see incarceration*
privilege 5–9, 33–34
punishment of children, physical, *see* Corporal punishment

race 8, 23, 33, 75–76, 94, 103
rape, *see Sexual Assault*
Reynolds, B. 61
Ridley, M. 68
romantic comedy xi, 60, 73
*Romeo and Juliet* 112
Rudman, L. 103
Ryan, M. 32

same-sex marriage 65, 71
Sanday, P. 44, 79
Sapolsky, R. 37–38
Sax., L. 23
Schwartznegger, A. 64
sex comparisons 13, 20–26, 28, 78
sex differences, *see* Sex comparisons
sexism 6, 9, 14–17, 19–21, 23–24, 30–32, 52–58, 64–65, 71, 79–80, 85–87, 94–96, 102–103, 117–120
sexual assault 5, 8, 30–31, 36, 41–44, 53–58, 65, 79–86, 89–95, 99, 104–07, 121–23
sexual harassment 31, 35, 58–59, 72–74, 79–80, 86–90, 95, 99, 118, 121–123
sexual orientation 5, 33, 43–44
sexuality 42–43, 51, 65
Sheen, C. 42
single-sex education 23

*social norms marketing* 53–55, 57, 86
sociobiology 39–42, 46–47
Speidel, L. 82
sports, *see Athletics*
Sprewell, L. 6
Stern, G. 89, 105, 107
Stice, E. 85
strip clubs 50–52, 55, 57–58, 65, 100, 111
suicide x, 4, 10, 97, 100, 112, 116
Summers, L. 21–23

Tavris, C. 42, 119
tempered radicals 99–100
Tennyson, A. 69
testosterone 25, 36–39
Thornhill, R. 41, 44
Title IX 22, 31–32
tonic immobility (freeze) response 39, 82
transgender people 1, 5
Treichler, P. 50
*Trouble with Testosterone, The* 37
Trump, D. 80

*unanimity effect* 57
"upstanders" 84, 93, 95

Valian, V. 23
Violence 4, 32, 37–39, 44–45, 69–70, 75–97, 99, 103, 116; against children 124–126; domestic (intimate partner) 8–10, 38, 78–79, 123; in media 76, 78, 95–96; offender characteristics 44, 79, 81–84, 92, 106; victim blaming 43, 82–83, 106–107

*Way We Never Were, The* 69
*Way We Really Are, The* 69
Weinstein, H. 72, 84
*When Harry met Sally* 32
White, E. 27
Williams, S. 12
Winfrey, O. 7
*Woman: An Intimate Geography* 42
Women's Studies 4
Wolsey, T. 60

zero-sum gender beliefs 10, 83, 120
Zimmerman, G. 75